TOMORROW'S WORLD TODAY

How the silicon chip works…
The fibre-optic global village…
Made-to-measure babies: a terrifying choice…
Nuclear power explained…
The future of space exploration…

This book examines more than fifty items from recent TOMORROW'S WORLD programmes and asks how these fascinating and important issues will develop and affect our future and what are their long-term implications.

Informative and compulsive reading for people of all ages.

About the author

David Filkin was appointed Editor of BBC television's TOMORROW'S WORLD in 1979 after more than fifteen years with the BBC, concentrating mainly on current affairs and documentary programmes on a wide range of subjects. TOMORROW'S WORLD TODAY is the first book to be published under his name, although he has written articles for the scientific press and acted as consultant on a series of scientific school library books.

TOMORROW'S WORLD TODAY

David Filkin

✦✦✦✦✦✦✦✦✦✦✦✦✦✦✦✦✦✦✦✦✦✦✦✦✦✦✦✦✦✦

*Illustrated by Alan Burton
Cartoons by Taffy Davies*

✦✦✦✦✦✦✦✦✦✦✦✦✦✦✦✦✦✦✦✦✦✦✦✦✦✦✦✦✦✦

BBC ♘

BBC/KNIGHT BOOKS

Copyright © British Broadcasting Corporation 1984
Illustrations © British Broadcasting Corporation/Knight Books 1984
First published by the British Broadcasting Corporation/Knight Books 1984

British Library C.I.P.

Filkin, David
    Tomorrow's world today.
    1. Technological innovations – Juvenile literature
    I. Title
    600   T173.8

    ISBN 0 340 33970 5
        (0 563 20199 1 BBC)

Origination by Planway Ltd., London N1.

Photoset by Rowland Phototypesetting Ltd., Bury St Edmunds, Suffolk.

Printed and bound in Great Britain by Hazell Watson & Viney Limited, Member of the BPCC Group, Aylesbury, Bucks.

Photo credits for TOMORROW'S WORLD TODAY

pp 8/9 Camera Press; **p. 11** Pekka Turunen; **p. 14** Dunlop Sports Company Ltd.; **p. 16** Paul Brierley; **p. 17** I.B.M. United Kingdom Ltd.; **p. 21** Truax Engineering Inc.; **p. 24** Camera Press; **p. 28** Camera Press; **p. 34** French Government Tourist Office; **p. 40** Scottish Farm Buildings Investigation Unit; **p. 41** Central Electricity Generating Board; **p. 43** Central Electricity Generating Board; **p. 45** United Kingdom Atomic Energy Authority; **p. 46** United Kingdom Atomic Energy Authority; **p. 48** Jet Joint Undertaking; **p. 53** Science Photo Library/Gene Cox; **p. 58** (Courtesy of) British Ceramic Research Association Ltd.; **p. 61 top** Motorola Inc. Semiconductor Product Division; **p. 61 bottom** Paul Brierley; **p. 62** Motorola Inc. Semiconductor Product Division; **p. 63** Motorola Inc. Semiconductor Product Division; **p. 64** Motorola Inc. Semiconductor Product Division; **p. 65** Paul Brierley; **pp. 68/69** Lucasfilm Ltd.; **p. 76** PHLS Centre for Applied Microbiology and Research; **p. 77** Science Photo Library/Dr Gopal Murti; **p. 80** Paul Brierley; **p. 86** Philips Electronics; **p. 87** Thorn EMI Lighting; **p. 89** Camera Press; **p. 92** Paul Brierley; **p. 97** David Ellis; **p. 100** Camera Press; **p. 101** Camera Press; **p. 102** Lockheed Missiles & Space Co. Inc.; **p. 104** Science Photo Library/A. R. Lawton; **p. 105** Science Photo Library/Science Source; **p. 108** Science Photo Library/Biology Media; **p. 112** Trinity House Lighthouse Service; **p. 113** United Wire Group & PA Technology; **p. 116** Science Photo Library/Nikoonahad; **p. 117** Science Photo Library/Nikoonahad; **pp. 120/121** Science Photo Library/Karl Esch; **p. 123** Elisabeth Photo Library; **p. 124** Science Photo Library/NASA

Contents

Is the Sun Still Shining?

It is no wonder that scientists are sometimes labelled "mad boffins" or "nutty professors". Surely no sensible person could look through the window on a sunny day and exclaim: "You know, the sun might not be shining any more!" Yet there are scientists who might have said that, and whose reasons have been published in the most respected of scientific journals, *Nature*. But how could the sun have stopped shining, when our eyes tell us it has not?

It is all to do with the evidence scientists now have about how the universe evolved. All the planets of our solar system were created by the chemistry, power and energy of our sun, forged in a furnace the equivalent of continually exploding hydrogen bombs. That energy, as sunlight, radiates across space to our planet. We can also calculate the complex physical equation that allows the hydrogen fusion to take place in the sun's interior, where all the energy and sunlight is produced. If you take three parts of hydrogen, drawn in from space, it should fuse together to produce one isotope of helium; plus a lot of other things to make the equation balance. Things such as photons – pure light energy; positrons – positive electrical energy; and neutrinos, a kind of spin energy to balance the positrons.

Scientists analysed the physical evidence to confirm this equation. They found all the hydrogen and helium that was needed: they even found rare elements like boron and berillium which they expected to be there, as by-products of the sun's nuclear reactions. But they just could not find enough neutrinos. A rather dull and uninteresting explanation could be that we got the equation wrong. But another possible explanation is that the nuclear reactions have stopped, and the sun is slowly dying down. But do not worry – there should still be plenty of sunlight for us. It will take another million years, fortunately,

for all the photons to work their way out from the sun's interior and so we will have sunlight for quite a while yet – even if the sun has stopped shining. Unless of course the sun stopped shining about a million years ago – and we have only just found out.

Pushing All Before It

In the days of the silent films, there were several classic moments of suspense which thrilled the audience – and the only sound was the tense music from the accompanying pianist inside the cinema. The train would be coming nearer, the heroine, bound firmly to the track with thick ropes, would struggle helplessly, the train would get closer and closer, the hero would arrive almost too late: and then at the last moment he would cut through her bonds and snatch the heroine away from within centimetres of the massive relentless steam train!

Nowadays train tracks are never blocked by beautiful film stars in distress; but there are a surprising number of regular obstructions on the line, from fallen trees to stray animals or even cars caught on a level crossing. With no cinema heroes to whisk them away, it struck a Finnish inventor that a novel way to clear the track could be fitted to the train front. If compressed gas is quickly released, a huge tough rubber balloon can be almost instantly inflated, providing an enormous cushion of air in front of the engine. This literally pushes an obstruction from

A cushion of air with split second precision lifts a test dummy clear of danger.

the lines in front of the train at the press of a button in the driver's cab. And it is so flexible that tests with dummies have shown that it can push a man from the track, and leave him little more than badly shaken and bruised.

It would be lovely to be able to report that the inflatable buffer could cope just as well with any conceivable kind of obstruction: but unfortunately it also succeeded in pushing a car on to the top of the engine. But the inventor is undeterred – he is convinced he can perfect the design soon. In the meantime, any heroines expecting to be tied to a railway track had better keep a traditional hero at the ready!

The Sticky Tape that Listens

Do you know how to listen to an earthworm exploring the bottom of a flower pot? Try the latest adhesive tape microphone! Any vibrating surface – however slightly it is moving – will disturb the air around it to produce a sound wave. The new microphone tape simply sticks to the side of, say, a flower pot and converts any vibrations in it into an electrical current

which is fed into conventional sound equipment. And when a worm in a flower pot moves – he can vibrate a flower pot a surprising amount!

Two stages in the delicate process of cooking the perfect tennis racquet.

Tennis à la Baked Alaska

If you have bought one of the latest kinds of tennis racquet, you might be forgiven if you can detect no connection between it and a very special ice-cream pudding – Baked Alaska. And as you drive a deep forehand over the net, you might confidently deny that both your racquet and the pudding are made in exactly the same way. But they are.

The trick in making a good Baked Alaska is to cover ice-cream with meringue mixture, and then pop it into a hot oven for just long enough to allow the meringue to cook without melting the ice-cream. And the trick in making the latest in nylon and carbon-fibre tennis racquets is just the same. Because the new compound racquet frame needs to be hollow if it is to match exactly the lightness, strength and feel of wooden racquets.

At first moulding the plastic frame in one piece, yet leaving it hollow, presented a problem. So scientists made a special metal core – the equivalent of the ice-cream in a Baked Alaska – with a low melting point: 160° Centigrade. The nylon and carbon-fibre mixture only melts at 260°C: and this is used like the meringue. The recipe is quite simple. First place the metal core inside a mould for the complete racquet; then pour in molten compound to surround the core completely and fill up the mould. Bake at 260°C for exactly two seconds to ensure the full blending of the compound and distribution around the mould, without melting the inner core. Remove and allow to cool. The mould is then opened, and the racquet removed, with a solid metal core still inside. Bake at only 200°C for fourteen minutes, and although the temperature is too low to re-melt the compound, it is high enough to melt the metal core – which flows out of the plastic racquet frame ready to be re-moulded as another racquet core. Game set and match to the chef!

Inside the Silicon Chip

Digital watches – space invaders – calculators and computers: all of them depend on the "chip". Most of us know that everything we do could soon be changed because of this one little bit of electronic circuitry: but how many of us know exactly what it is or how it works?

Think for a minute about a digital watch – to tell the time it switches on a series of electrically produced numbers one after the other. A tiny piece of quartz crystal makes sure that every second precisely a new number is switched on. But how does the watch know which number to show when? And how to do complicated things like change the minute number every sixty seconds, the hour number every sixty minutes, the date every twenty-four hours, the month every thirty-one days – or thirty days depending on the month – or twenty-eight days in February – or twenty-nine days in February in a leap year?

The silicon chip can do all that. Because all it is in effect is an incredibly tiny switching centre.

The microchip – at work. The active parts are no thicker than a human hair.

A very powerful – 64k – microchip makes a paperclip look gigantic.

A battery sends out a tiny electrical current around a circuit of switches, changing them as it goes. If no switches are in the "on" position the display on the watch might read something like "00 hours: 00 minutes: 00 seconds." With the aid of the quartz crystal which makes sure that a change happens exactly every second, the current from the battery makes the first change; by, say, switching one switch "on" leaving all the rest "off". This makes the watch read "00 hours: 00 minutes: 01 seconds." A second later, the current switches another switch "on". The two "on" switches make the watch read "00: 00: 02." For the next second, "00: 00: 03", the current might perhaps switch the first switch back off again; for "00: 00: 04" it could switch on switch number three, leaving switch number two on, with switch one still "off". And so on. A whole number of switch positions are set up by the current, second by second, so that a different number is displayed on the watch for each combination of positions.

When the watch shows "00: 00: 59" something a bit different happens, because the silicon chip contains a special switch that comes into operation at that time. This switch opens up a new circuit which changes the minutes on the watch – just as with the seconds – by electrically switching on or off several switches; it also switches off all the switches in the circuit for the seconds and lets the current start changing those numbers every second all over again. So the watch display changes from "00: 00: 59" to "00: 01: 00" when a minute is reached. The special minutes circuit is then switched off while the seconds circuit counts up to 59 again. At "00: 01: 59" the minutes circuit is opened up again – and "00: 02: 00" is displayed. At "00: 59: 59", a third circuit is switched in – to count the hours: and the display changes to "01: 00: 00". Then the counting starts all over again.

And at every significant point in time beyond this, all the silicon chip has to do is to switch in another special circuit: so that every twenty-four hours the date changes, and a new number for the day is displayed. If the month on display is January, March, May, July, August, October or December, the days count to thirty-one before the month changes: for the other months, except February, the switch system ensures that the month changes after thirty days. And depending on whether a leap year is on display or not, a special circuit of switches makes sure that February has twenty-eight or twenty-nine days as appropriate.

Obviously, even in a watch there must be an incredible number of switches to let you make all the changes you need to keep changing everything on display. That's why the silicon chip is so marvellous. Because in one little thin piece of silicon, no bigger than your finger nail, you can have a highly complicated electrical circuit containing thousands of switches. It doesn't start that small of course: the electronics expert who designs the circuits can spend days and days planning and drawing the circuits and all the switches. These are then "copied" – a bit like having it photographed – on to special materials which allow it to be first miniaturised – rather like the opposite of enlarging a print from a photograph negative – and then chemically transferred to the silicon, with all the circuit lines and switches printed into it. One set of chemicals completely covers the silicon so that electricity cannot flow through it; and another set of chemicals then dissolves away this protective layer of chemicals only along the lines of the circuits, making it possible for electricity to go around the circuits. And the whole process gives you the equivalent of a photographic negative. Once you have made one silicon chip it is quite easy to make thousands and thousands of exact copies: so digital watches, calculators and so on become cheaper and cheaper. Computers used to need so many switches and circuits that, only a few years ago, they took up a whole building, now they can be built no bigger than a television set. The work that silicon chips can do is fantastic, and still being explored. For a start they are being used to help plan and draw the circuits for other silicon chips!

Anything involving straightforward decisions can be programmed on to a silicon chip – a switch in the "on" position could mean "yes" and in the "off" position "no". It is quite easy to programme a chip in a watch to play "Happy Birthday To You" for instance. Every time the date changes on your watch, a little circuit like this could receive an electric current. Pretend your birthday is 20 July.

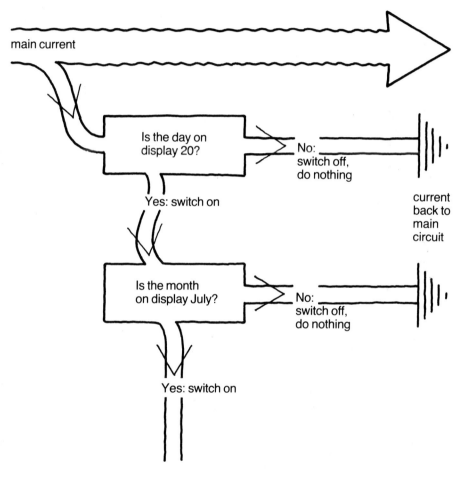

main current

Is the day on display 20?

No: switch off, do nothing

current back to main circuit

Yes: switch on

Is the month on display July?

No: switch off, do nothing

Yes: switch on

Activate circuit of switches to play musical notes of 'Happy Birthday to You' in sequence

Now – can you fill in the details you need to make a special circuit to set an alarm clock off at 07: 30: 00?

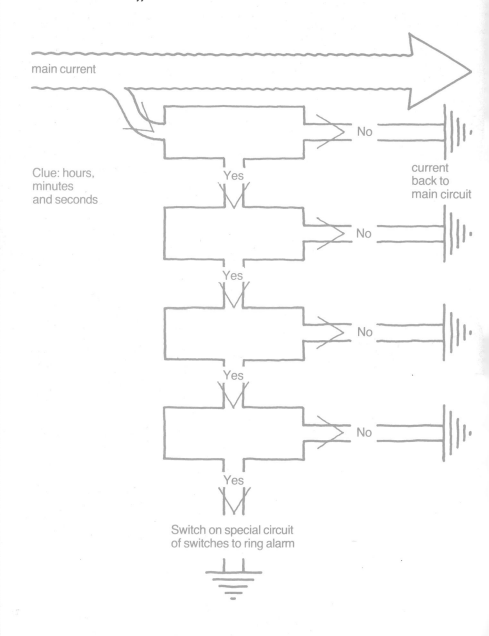

main current

Clue: hours, minutes and seconds

No

Yes

current back to main circuit

No

Yes

No

Yes

No

Yes

Switch on special circuit of switches to ring alarm

Finally, try to design your own circuits.
How about one which rings a bell on the first of each month, weekends and Christmas Day? Think about it!

There's a Rocket in the Garden

What hobbies does your neighbour have? Does he grow roses in his back garden? Or keep pigeons? Unless you live in California's Santa Cara county, in Green Meadow Lane, Saratoga to be precise, you are unlikely to have a neighbour quite like Bob Truax. Because in *his* back garden, he is building a fully practical, one man, space rocket. He has got clearance to launch it from his local airport once it is fully tested; and it will not have cost him as much to build as you might have imagined. His helium containers for instance are titanium pressure vessels once used on Titan missiles, produced at a cost of ten thousand dollars each; but as obsolete military scrap each one cost Bob Truax fifty dollars. His navigation system is an auto pilot, developed for the X-15 rocket plane at a staggering cost of twenty-five million dollars. He bought three of the only four ever made, at the incredible price of thirty-six dollars each. In a flight to the edge of space, his astronaut will have no special oxygen supply for the 100-mile round trip: it will last only five minutes, and Bob reckons there will be ample air in the cockpit. And it is not deterring any would-be astronauts. Bob has a waiting list of two hundred who want to make the flight.

Bob Truax with his homemade spacecraft.

21

Listen to Life

People who love plants will sometimes tell you that they have to talk to them nicely to make them flourish! But even if you believe that, are you ready for this: a good way to see what energy a plant is using is to listen to it! Not that the plant can speak in English or in any other language. But with the help of a technique called photo-acoustic spectrometry you can get a very accurate picture of the wavelengths of light which a plant absorbs as energy to help it grow.

I SAY... WOULD YOU MIND TURNING YOUR RHUBARB DOWN A BIT....?!

You start with a light source shone through a prism – which splits the white light into all the colours of the rainbow which make it. Each of these colours is put in front of the plant in turn, and the living cells respond to each colour differently. A microphone can hear the cells absorb light and synthesise it with carbon, because the carbon heats up as it absorbs light. This heat makes the air next to the plant move, as a sound wave. The hotter the carbon, the more light energy is being used, and the louder the sound. At the blue end of the light spectrum, hardly any light is absorbed by the plant – and there is hardly any sound; but as you move through the spectrum, different plants give you different sounds, showing exactly how each one uses light.

This fascinating technique of photo-acoustic spectrometry is also extremely useful in other fields, from helping to design laser mirrors to analysing blood stains. It is even hoped it may help us to detect some of the differences in living cells and give us clues to the way in which cancer develops.

Divers in Disneyland

The special voices Walt Disney dreamed up for Mickey Mouse and Donald Duck just might not have been totally original ideas: if, that is, the king of cartoons had ever been deep-sea diving. Because strangely enough, the voices of divers from far below the surface sound eerily like Donald or Mickey. That is because of the way divers at depth have to breathe. If they tried to breathe the ordinary air that suits all of us at the surface, the enormous pressure of the water deep down in the ocean would make it impossible for their lungs to suck it in. It would be rather like trying to drink treacle through a straw. So the air a diver breathes is specially "thinned" with a very light gas – such as helium. And helium affects the vocal chords – quite harmlessly – making the diver speak with a squeaky little voice. But helium is a very expensive gas; and when a diver breathes out, it simply bubbles back to the surface of the sea and is wasted.

So, with more and more men needed to work on the ocean bed – in the oil industry for instance – a way to recycle the helium had to be found.

One new system does this with simple chemicals and collection bags. Helium and oxygen are mixed in exactly the right proportions in one bag with the help of a special pressure sensor. The diver breathes in the mixture, and breathes it out into another bag. Now the gas mixture in that bag contains some unused oxygen, the helium, and some carbon dioxide produced when the diver used up some of the oxygen. So this gas mixture is fed through a container of soda lime, which removes the carbon dioxide; and then the gases left are fed back to the first bag. There the correct levels of oxygen and helium are mixed again by topping up with new gas from the supply cylinders. All of which should ensure that cartoon voices reach the control teams on board diving vessels as cheaply and efficiently as possible.

It is both expensive and difficult to do a really deep dive yourself. Not only do you need special equipment and training to prepare yourself for the way the pressure will affect you; you also have to have a complete support team of expert divers to monitor your progress and make sure you do not go down or come up again too quickly. That is because of the way the pressure changes as you go deeper or shallower. Next time you have a bath, try this experiment. You need a balloon, a rubber band and a long hollow tube.

Fix the balloon very securely on to one end of the tube with a rubber band.

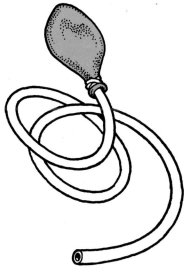

Blow it up as hard as you can, out of the water. Remember how hard or easy it was, then let it deflate. Now put the balloon under the water and try to blow it up from above the surface by blowing down the tube.

Is it easier or harder than it was when the balloon was above the water? It is the pressure of the water on the balloon which makes the difference; and unless something was done to help him, a diver's lungs would be affected in a similar way.

Getting in the Groove

Just every so often, science and technology has a habit of turning itself upside down. Take sound reproduction. In an age of tape recorders and cassettes, Dolby noise reduction systems and digital recording, the last thing you would expect anyone to turn topsy turvy is the way the good old gramophone record is played. Instead of spinning the record forty-five or thirty-three and a third times a minute on a turntable – why not keep the record *still*, and drive an amplifier and speaker, linked to a stylus, from the outside groove to the inside, by letting it all circle round and round the disc at exactly the right speed? A Japanese engineer set himself the challenge of producing this new record-playing system and came across some interesting problems. First he built a model van into which speaker and amplifier were installed, together with a motor to drive the van's wheels. But how could he make the model move in ever decreasing circles towards the middle of the record? The answer was to let the needle or stylus dictate the *path* of the van, and use the motor to power only one wheel to help it keep going in circles. So the needle was set into the bottom of the van, not only to transfer vibrations from the grooves of the record, but also to follow them faithfully and take the van along them. But then another problem emerged. A turning record plays at a constant speed: so the stylus takes longer to complete a circuit of the record at its outside edge where the grooves are in bigger circles, than at the centre, where the grooves are in much smaller circles. For the model van to reproduce the music accurately, it had to be slowed down as it travelled round those smaller and smaller circles of grooves. As the turning circle of the van gets tighter, the angle of the control arm holding the stylus has to become sharper: so this change in position of the control arm is used to regulate the speed of the motor. In fact there is only one snag with this model van record player: it simply does not produce music as well as the traditional gramophone – so nobody wants it for more than a novelty.

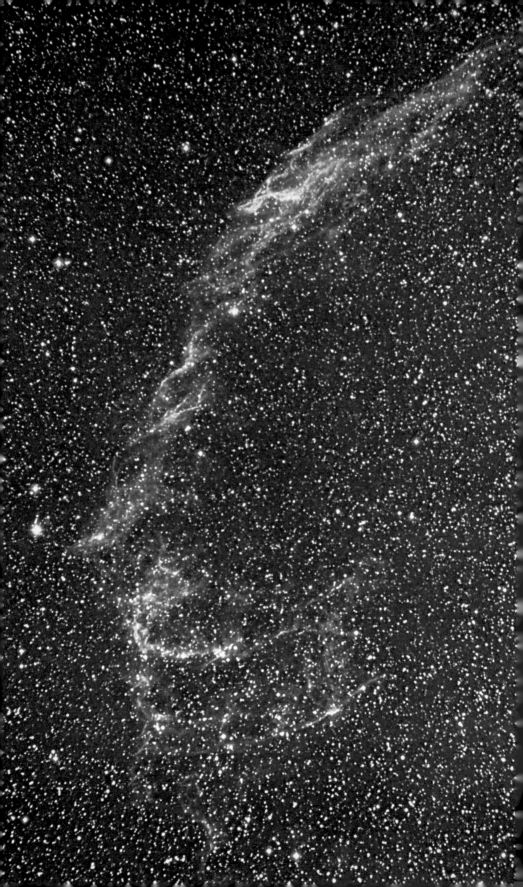

The Infinite Universe

Think of a huge number: then double it. Then double it again – and again – and again. And before you lose track of the massive number you are creating, imagine doubling up numbers for ever. Even supposing you could actually do so, you would never reach infinity. Because infinity is not really a number: it is simply a word to describe what happens if you go on for ever. You could take an infinite journey around a circle for instance – because there is no beginning or end to a circle. And once you have grasped the meaning of infinity, then some pretty amazing ideas become possible. To begin with – how far can you see? Look up into the sky at night, and you will see stars which astronomers know are just some of the thousand million stars in our galaxy. And that galaxy is itself just a tiny part of the universe. As for the universe – well presumably that just goes on for ever. Or does it? If we cannot even see beyond our own galaxy, how can we tell whether the universe is infinite – or whether it just comes to some kind of an end? Is it round, like a sphere? Is it flat? Or just shapeless and endless?

We can of course, look further into the universe than our naked eyes can see. Huge powerful telescopes help us to do that. But some unusual things start to happen when you consider looking further and further into space. Nothing we know of travels faster than light – it travels at almost eighteen million kilometres a minute. This means that virtually all we can see is available to our senses almost at the instant we look at it. But if we could somehow build a telescope powerful enough to see a star about forty-eight billion kilometres away, then its light would be rushing towards earth at over nine billion kilometres a year – so that the light from the star would take five years to reach us. When you saw the star through the telescope it would not be as it is now, but as it was five years ago.

Now, imagine being able to see billions and billions of kilometres further away still. Even if we could ever create telescopes to do so, we could never see anything more than sixteen thousand million billion kilometres away. Because the light travelling from something so far away would take so long to travel to us, that it would have to have begun its journey before the "big bang" took place. That is the time when astronomers have calculated a colossal explosion of energy must have taken place, to give birth to at least a million million galaxies, all with their millions of stars. In other words, the light travelling from something sixteen thousand million billion kilometres away which reaches us now must have started its journey before there was anything to see – because nothing had been created!

But since the astronomers managed to calculate how long ago the "big bang" took place (by studying the movement and speed of the planets and other matter in space) it is perhaps not so surprising that they can also use their observations to calculate other things about the universe. For instance they have worked out the reason why the planets revolve around the sun, and their moons revolve around the planets. It may sound incredible, but it is because the weight of the sun actually *bends* space. It is easier to understand this if you imagine a "slice" of space: in this experiment the rubber sheeting represents the slice. You need a cylinder and enough rubber sheeting to spread over one end, and two different-sized balls.

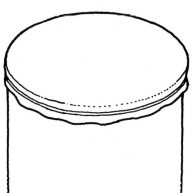

Stretch the rubber skin over the end of the cylinder like a drum, and fasten in place.

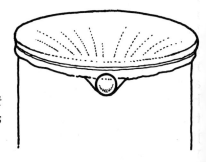

Drop a cricket ball in the middle and it "bends space" as it sinks and stretches the rubber.

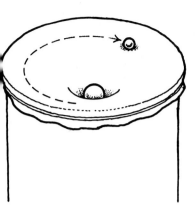

Now roll a smaller ball – say a golf ball – around the inside of the stretched skin. It will circle the cricket ball just like a planet orbiting the sun.

Every star is just another sun, probably with a solar system all its own. If every star, and all its planets and their moons were loaded into space, the weight of all the matter in the universe would gradually stretch space more and more. Eventually our "drumskin" would completely encircle all the galaxies inside it. You can't produce the effect with the rubber sheet because it would tear before the weight was sufficient, but the sequence is rather like that of a drip of water forming on a tap and eventually becoming a complete sphere-like drop.

That could be one way to explain the shape of the universe. It is a matter of complicated mathematics for the scientists to work out just how many stars and planets and moons and asteroids and so on it needs for space to be bent into a balloon-like universe. It would be an infinite universe – because travelling around inside it, your journey would never end. You would go on making circular tours for ever and ever.

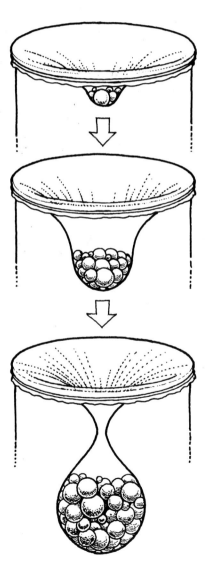

But there is one very basic problem about accepting this explanation of the universe. The physicists simply have not discovered enough matter – whether stars, planets, moons or anything else – in the universe to make space bend right round into a balloon shape. So another kind of infinite universe has to be a possibility – one where the weight of the galaxies only bends space; it is never fully enclosed and must simply go on for ever and ever. Like doubling up numbers can go on for ever and ever. And if you go on doing anything for ever, for an infinite number of times, strange possibilities come up. When you toss a coin it comes down heads or tails. If you tossed a coin millions of times it would come down heads or tails each time. But tossing a coin an *infinite* number of times must allow for the strangest of possibilities to come true – because anything that is infinite must include *all* possibilities, however unlikely. So it means the coin *could* come down on its edge, for instance, as one of an infinite number of possibilities. In the same way, in an infinite universe without end, all possibilities must occur. And in theory that means that somewhere in the universe there could be another person, exactly like you, reading another book, exactly like this!

If that all sounds a little too far-fetched to be true, then the other more sensible theory of the universe needs a lot of hard work by the astronomers. Because to make a closed-in universe they have yet to find five times more stars than we already know about. It makes doubling up numbers for ever seem quite simple!

Getting a Bounce out of Warmth

Why on earth should anyone want to spend time and effort making a little box with a heater in it – just to warm up a squash ball? The answer is that the bounce of the ball changes as the ball gets warm – and in a good game of squash the belting of the ball by the players soon warms it up if it is cold to start with. So in order to be sure that the ball bounces consistently throughout an important match, the players need to start with a ball that's already warm.

Scientific Wine

If you ask most expert wine tasters, they will tell you that French vineyards have for many years produced the world's finest red wines. Whether you prefer Bordeaux or Burgundy wines, you can be sure that generations of special skills and experience have gone into the intricate details involved in wine production. In one vineyard, the grapes will be picked when only just ripe; in another, they will be allowed to become so ripe that they start to ferment while still on the vine. Burgundies are made from one grape variety only – the Pinot Noir: Bordeaux wines are blended from three or four varieties – Cabernet, Merlot and Mabee for instance. And, according to the weather and the condition of the soil, wines from the same vineyard can vary in quality, taste and strength from one year to the next. Skilled winemakers will be able to judge how long to keep a wine before drinking it, because the wine continues to mature in the bottle. Many of the best wines are worth keeping for ten, twenty or even more years before drinking them. And it is the traditional skills of French families, passed on from generation to generation, that has ensured that the finest possible wines are produced there year by year.

The traditional French approach to good wine owes little to the laboratory.

When the Californians decided to step up the production of quality wines only twenty-five years ago, they did not have all those years of experience to teach them how to make the most of their grapes. So they turned to science for help. Because, although they could copy much of the French tradition – for instance, importing all the same grape varieties from France when planting their vineyards – somehow they were just not getting the same quality wines. They analysed their soils, then ran tests on the local pinewood barrels in which the wines were fermented, and they tried to calculate the effect of differences in the wind. They needed to know how quickly it made vine leaves give up evaporated moisture, because this affects the acid levels in the grapes. And to analyse the differences in the grape juices at each stage of development, they used a technique called high-pressure liquid chromatography. A sample of grape juice is mixed with a plastic resin which reacts with different acids in the juice: under ultra-violet light, each acid will absorb different levels of light. These can be measured electronically, and the wine-maker can see precisely how much

BOTTLE № 17421
"AN UNASSUMING.
LITTLE
WINE........☐"

of each acid is present in the grape juice at each stage of its production. If the acid levels differ from the ideal levels detected in a French wine at the same stage, then specially isolated bacteria can be added to the fermentation process to readjust the balance.

The results of this scientific approach to wine making are becoming more impressive each year: and some wine experts are now saying that there are Californian wines which are worthy rivals to their best French equivalents.

Growing Hydrogen

The trouble with nearly all our fuels is the pollution they cause. That is why so many of the world's cities now have strict laws about what fuels can be used and how factories get rid of fumes. Yet there is one fuel that just could not be cleaner – because all it leaves when it burns is water. That fuel is hydrogen. In its liquid form, it is one of the essential sources of energy for all space craft, including the Shuttle. Yet it has hardly been used at all to power other vehicles – primarily because it is so expensive. Although it would not cause pollution, hydrogen cannot be produced cheaply enough to replace conventional fuels.

And yet everywhere, hydrogen is being extracted from water all the time, by plants. Millions of them manage it effortlessly. It is all part of the process by which they live and grow. The trouble is that the hydrogen is not released by the plants in any way and so we cannot farm it.

Plants absorb water through their roots. It then travels through the stem of the plant into the leaves. There, inside individual living cells in the leaves, energy from the sun splits the water into oxygen and hydrogen, and the oxygen is released back into the atmosphere. The hydrogen is transferred to other parts of the plant where it combines with carbon dioxide and other chemicals to produce new material for the plant, so it can develop and thrive. If we could somehow *interrupt* this natural process at the point where the hydrogen is produced from water, we would have a cheap supply of the perfect fuel. Scientists at King's College London have been working on this basis. First, they have managed to isolate the part of the living plant cell which captures solar energy to make the hydrogen. These parts are called chloroplasts, and they can only exist outside a living plant for a few hours before they die. But during that time, scientists have managed to mix chloroplasts with suitable chemicals as catalysts, and convert water into hydrogen and oxygen. The hydrogen can be collected from this artificial production line – but only slowly in very small quantities. What the researchers at King's College hope to do next is to find ways to speed up the release of the hydrogen from the chloroplast mixture, and to see if they can keep the chloroplasts alive longer. And they are also trying another idea. By analysing the chloroplasts, they have been able to synthesise mixtures of chemicals which can produce hydrogen by absorbing light.

What a hydrogen factory of the future might look like.

In the long run, the hope is that by combining chloroplasts and other chemicals in some kind of jelly, we will be able to float huge artificial leaves on lakes, reservoirs, or even oceans; and from them harvest hydrogen in abundance. That day is a long way off yet – but if it means an end to the scars on the landscape so often left by coal mines, power stations and oil rigs, as well as the cleanest fuel possible for all our energy needs, then it is certainly worth working for.

Fake Steak

You rarely get steak for school dinners because it is so expensive. Only cheaper cuts of beef would be within a school's meal budget: but often these can be really tough to chew. So how about a process to give you tender steaks for dinner, not from the best cuts of meat, not even from the poorer cuts, but actually from the gristle and bits that are usually thrown away?

A new machine which does that is a bit like a mechanical sieve. It works on the principle that lean meat is much softer than gristle. At a carefully controlled rate, chopped up chunks of gristly meat are pressed into the sieve. The softer lean meat is pushed through, not as mince, but as uncut long strands of chewy, meaty, lean beef. The gristle that has been separated

MY COMPLIMENTS
TO THE RESEARCH
CHEMIST........

out is then removed and chopped up into tiny edible pieces. And the two separated ingredients are then used to make artificial steaks from real meat. The red lean strands are compressed together, then surrounded by a layer of fat and chopped gristle. The whole thing is frozen and can be sawn into real-looking steaks. More important, a panel of schoolboy experts thought they tasted just as good too.

Mabel, the Bionic Cow

IT'S NOTHING SERIOUS....SHE'S JUST BLOWN A COUPLE OF FUSES....

VET

Tread carefully if you spend a summer's day hiking in the fields of Aberdeenshire. Because there is one cow which will not step aside as you stride towards her. Her name is Mabel – and she is no ordinary cow. Instead of flesh and blood, she is all wiring and gauges – although her cow hide is remarkably like that of her livelier sisters. This unique machine is designed to feel the weather like any other cow – and the circuitry inside it

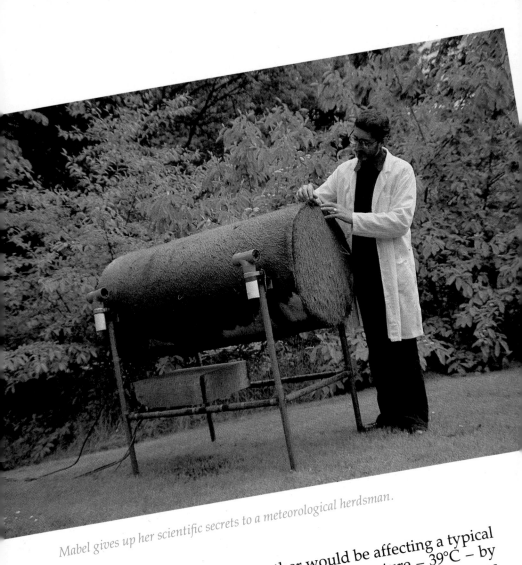

Mabel gives up her scientific secrets to a meteorological herdsman.

measures exactly how the weather would be affecting a typical cow. Mabel is kept at the ideal cow temperature – 39°C – by electrical energy driving a hot air fan, and how much she uses each day is compared with the wind and rainfall, sunshine and even snow all around her, measured painstakingly twenty-four hours a day. And Mabel does not do all this to satisfy some eccentric engineer's desire to make an electronic cow: she has been designed to tell farmers how much energy, in terms of food stuffs, is needed to meet their cows' needs without waste. So if you want to know how to make a cow really happy – ask Mabel.

What is Nuclear Power?

It is hard to imagine that a simple glass of water contains an abundance of energy, if only we could get it out! But that is just what a nuclear power station does: it releases the energy which binds together all the particles which make up single

The fuelling machine of a nuclear reactor is housed in this colossal hall.

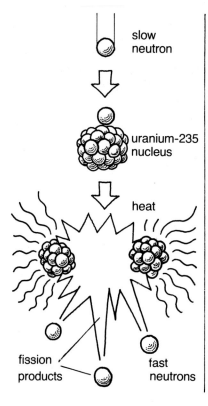

slow neutron

uranium-235 nucleus

heat

fission products

fast neutrons

How nuclear fission works.

atoms of a chemical. Water is made up of two chemicals – hydrogen and oxygen: it contains atoms of both, which could in theory be split into tiny particles, releasing energy.

To understand how a drop of still water can be full of energy, think of a rugby scrum. All the men in it are pushing hard, so there is a lot of energy there; but if both teams are equally strong and well-balanced, nothing moves. The energy is concentrated on keeping all the players tightly packed together. As soon as one or two players stop pushing, however, the whole scrum starts moving and perhaps breaks up, with players falling or running off as their energy is released.

The process of splitting an atom to release its energy is called nuclear fission. Imagine one extra rugby player barging in at a well-balanced scrum: he could knock it off balance and break it up, releasing other rugby players. If each of them then barged into other rugby scrums and broke them up, then the players released could break up even more rugby scrums – and so on. There would be a chain reaction, releasing more and more energy as it continued.

In nuclear fission, one particle, or bit of an atom, is used to smash an atom into – say – four particles. Each of them then breaks up four atoms – which will release sixteen particles – and in no time thousands of atoms are being split, releasing a huge amount of energy. This is exactly how a nuclear bomb explosion happens: it is an *uncontrolled* chain reaction of collisions. And because it is so destructive and powerful, a lot of people confuse the nuclear bomb with nuclear power: and are frightened that nuclear power must be just as dangerous.

In fact nuclear power does involve dangerous materials, and whether the problems of handling those materials can be justified is still a matter for debate, but it is important to understand that nuclear power stations do not involve uncontrolled chain reactions like the bomb. All the reactions are *controlled*.

The atoms which are to be smashed are usually uranium. This is chosen because it is already radioactive: in other words, particles are naturally breaking away from the atom even before a chain reaction is started. This makes it easier to smash the atom and release its energy. The uranium is prepared for the nuclear reactor by making it into pellets which are put into long rods. The rods are known as the fuel elements. They can be moved into and out of the part of the reactor where particles are released: these particles need atoms to break up, and the uranium pellets provide those atoms to "fuel" the nuclear reaction. If the reaction starts to get too fast, with so many atoms being split at once that the chain reaction could become too powerful, the special control rods are pushed back into the reactor core. They absorb particles, and so with fewer particles to cause the nuclear fission, it slows down and then the control rods can be withdrawn from the reactor core once more. In this way the reaction is controlled, and is neither too fast nor too slow. The energy is released in the form of heat: so it is a simple matter to use a thermostat to lower the control rods when the reaction produces a temperature above the safe level, and to raise the control rods when the temperature falls too low.

Preparing the fuel rods for a nuclear reactor.

The heat from this controlled reaction is then transferred, using either a gas or water as what is called the coolant, to a more conventional kind of power generator – a turbine. The heat is used to produce steam which turns the blades of the turbine to produce electricity.

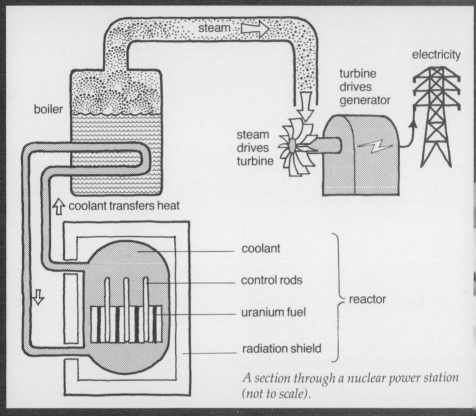

A section through a nuclear power station (not to scale).

People in favour of nuclear power stations maintain that it is cheaper to produce heat this way than by burning coal or oil. They argue that the reactors can be made acceptably safe with automatic "shut down" arrangements which will come into effect if anything goes wrong. The control rods would, in that instance, be automatically dropped into the reactor core; the reaction could not continue because there would be no fuel. But people who argue against nuclear power say that however thorough such precautions may be, there is a very real danger caused by the high levels of radioactivity involved.

Radioactivity itself is no more dangerous or unusual than heat. It is all around us. Milk and beer are measurably radioactive, but they do us no harm. The level of radioactivity is acceptable to our bodies – just as the heat from a hot water bottle is perfectly harmless. On the other hand, just as there are levels of heat – such as a naked flame or boiling water – which can damage us, so there are levels of radioactivity that can harm our bodies. It is all a question of degree. Uranium in its natural state is harmless enough for us to pick up uranium ore: the number of particles breaking away is so relatively small that they do not do us any damage. Increase the number of particles breaking off, in other words raise the level of radioactivity, and there is more danger. Then these particles will bombard and change the structure of living cells. At a controlled level of radioactivity, this can be useful: doctors use radioactivity to destroy some kinds of cancer cells, for instance, because they are more easily changed and destroyed than healthy cells. But if the level of radioactivity is too high, then healthy cells too can be destroyed. And then a person can become seriously ill, and sometimes die.

In a nuclear reactor, the relatively harmless low levels of radioactivity in the uranium fuel pellets are not difficult to handle. But during the nuclear reaction, as the atoms of uranium are broken up, they form particles which do not simply break up more atoms of uranium. Some of the particles join up with each other to make new substances, some of which are very unstable and last only for a very short time; others last longer. The general rule is that the shorter time the substance lasts, the more highly radioactive it will be. And very highly radioactive, potentially lethal substances are created in a nuclear reactor. After it has been used, every fuel rod will still contain a lot of uranium, plus a large number of other radioactive materials, including some very dangerous ones, which are of no use any more. These are known as nuclear waste. Special care has to be taken to remove the nuclear waste in order to re-use the unspent uranium; and then the nuclear waste has to be disposed of. This is a real problem, because although the most highly radioactive waste is so unstable that it will quickly break up, or decay, there are some dangerously radioactive substances which will last for many years.

A modern nuclear reactor being fuelled with fresh uranium.

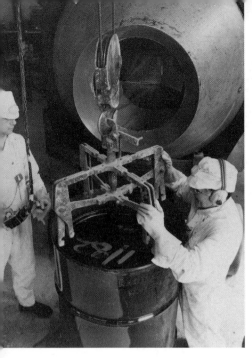

One kind of nuclear waste being prepared for encasing in concrete prior to disposal at sea.

Supporters of nuclear power say that the waste can be safely handled. First of all it is stored in cooling ponds of water, then in liquid form in tanks. Once the shorter lived, high-level radioactive materials have decayed, the remaining – still dangerous – radioactive waste can be processed and safely buried, they argue. A favourite scheme at the moment is to seal the waste in glass so thick that it cannot be easily destroyed.

The opponents of nuclear power argue that the waste stays dangerous for so long that we cannot guarantee any method of containing it: they suggest that earthquakes, or deliberate terrorist activities for instance, could release the highly radioactive waste. And they also argue that if a power station failed, or was destroyed by terrorists or some terrible accident, then the highly radioactive wastes in the reactor core could be released.

All over the world, governments are trying to decide just how safe nuclear power has to be to justify its use. With conventional fuels like coal, oil and gas being used faster than we can discover new supplies – and certainly faster than nature can create new stock piles – it is very tempting to see nuclear power as a long term cheap alternative source of energy. But many people remain unconvinced that the industry can handle nuclear waste safely enough, and that nuclear reactors will ever be secure enough. New ideas are constantly being tested but it is still impossible to tell whether we will ever have nuclear powered electricity as confidently on supply as our tap water.

Nuclear Fusion

It did not take long for scientists to realise, after they had split the atom to release lots of energy, that the reverse process could also produce energy. Instead of using particles to break up existing atoms, why not find a way to force atoms together, to create a new atom and release energy at the same time? Hydrogen has an ideal atom for the process, because we know that atoms of hydrogen fuse together in the sun to produce helium, and to create all the power and energy we receive on earth as sunlight. And if we can mimic this nuclear fusion, as it is called, then we will have a much "cleaner" process than nuclear fission, the process of creating energy by splitting atoms. Nuclear fusion would not create all the radioactive waste which nuclear fission produces, and which is a problem to get rid of.

But fusing atoms is far from easy. The atoms have a basic stability and it takes a huge amount of energy to break this down. At present, it is still not practically possible to get more energy out of a fusion reaction than is put into it in the first place. Under high enough pressures and at a high enough temperature, which both take energy, atoms have been made to fuse: but only for a fraction of a

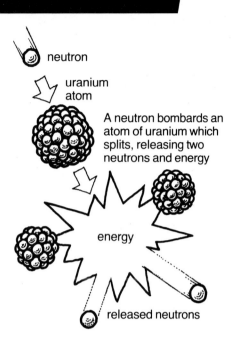

neutron

uranium atom

A neutron bombards an atom of uranium which splits, releasing two neutrons and energy

energy

released neutrons

The principles of nuclear fission . . . compared with nuclear fusion.

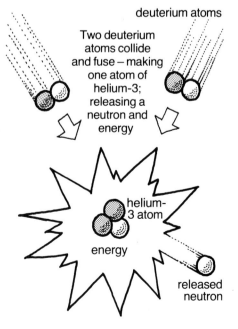

deuterium atoms

Two deuterium atoms collide and fuse – making one atom of helium-3; releasing a neutron and energy

helium-3 atom

energy

released neutron

The ring of magnets which will contain the plasma for nuclear fusion experiments at Culham in Oxfordshire, England.

second. There is no chain reaction, and so no continuous source of heat.

The difficulties start because the hydrogen gas will only be ready to fuse when it is so hot that the atoms are separated into negative electrons and positively charged nuclei. At normal temperatures, the negative electrical charge of the electron and the positive electrical charge of the nucleus bind them firmly together like the north and south poles of two powerful magnets. It takes a temperature of about 100,000,000 degrees centigrade to separate them, and then overcome the natural tendency of the positively charged nuclei to repel each other – like the two south poles of two magnets – so that those nuclei can fuse together and release energy. And at that temperature, the gas, or plasma, as it is called when it is so hot, is extremely difficult to contain. You cannot simply hold it in a physical container: the heat would melt the container, and the plasma is so fluid that it will escape through most materials anyway, like water going through a filter paper.

One way to contain the plasma is to use the very electrical or magnetic forces which bind the nuclei and the electrons together. If you can build the right kind of magnetic field all around the plasma, with strong enough forces to repel the particles, then you can push the plasma back, or contain it, within the magnetic field, if it tries to escape. It is a bit like trying to contain a few handfuls of air so that you can press them together to make something really solid. You cannot easily grasp the air, but you can push it, a bit at a time, through a valve into a rubber leakproof container which is itself inside a non-stretching cover. This happens when you inflate a football; the air contained under pressure makes it feel really solid. In nuclear fusion, a ring of electromagnets creates a magnetic field that is like the two bags of the football, and the plasma is the equivalent of the air kept contained within the football. You need a ring of electromagnets in pairs to contain plasma: because if you simply let plasma flow between two magnets it gets "pinched" or squeezed in at the middle (see diagram A).

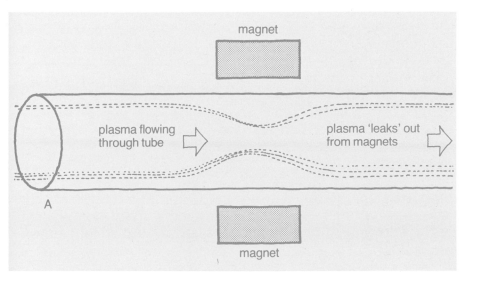

magnet

plasma flowing through tube

plasma 'leaks' out from magnets

A

magnet

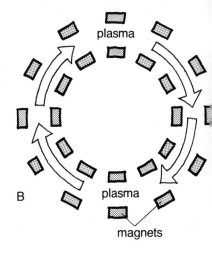

plasma

B

plasma

magnets

Obviously that will only contain the plasma at the "sides" – it can still "leak out" at the end of the magnets. So you need to build a circle of magnets which will induce the plasma to go round and round the circle, like a toy train on a track, without ever finding an end to "leak" out of (see diagram B). This kind of plasma container is called a Taurus, and several of these huge rings of magnets have been built in Russia and America particularly. In Britain, at Culham in Berkshire, many European countries have joined together to build the latest one, called JET.

With JET the scientists are hoping to discover the problems of creating and containing the high temperatures at which fusion takes place. There is no plan to try to develop a practical system to generate electricity yet.

But using magnets to compress and contain the plasma may not be the best solution. While the power of the magnets puts the plasma under pressure, it also heats it. (Feel how hot your bicycle pump becomes while you are blowing up a football or tyre quickly.) So why not approach the problem the other way round, and heat materials so rapidly that they become a plasma and allow fusion to take place, before the plasma can escape? One way to attempt that is to bombard a mixture of deuterium and tritium from all sides with immensely powerful lasers. If the deuterium and tritium are heated quickly to a very high temperature, they are transformed into the right kind of plasma for fusion to take place. But this takes so much laser power that it is almost impossible to handle the lasers. And the plasma is hard to contain long enough for fusion to take place. It all happens in a fraction of a second – and so the whole problem of how to produce a chain reaction for a continuous supply of energy would have to be overcome, even if laser fusion was easily organised.

So it looks as though we are still a long way off from producing energy through nuclear fusion. If we can succeed, though, it could solve all the arguments about our present nuclear power stations, as nuclear waste would no longer be a problem.

There are several ways you can appreciate some of the principles involved in trying to harness energy through nuclear fusion.

First, get hold of two bar magnets and place them end to end. What happens? If they attract and stick together, you have got two "opposite" poles of the magnets together. If they repel each other, you have got two "like" magnetic poles, either two norths or two souths. You can tell which by letting the magnets swing freely on the end of a string and seeing which end points north and which points south. The electrical properties of particles which are either positively or electrically charged means they behave in the same way as the magnets. "Like" poles or electrical charges repel each other: "opposite" poles attract. But while you can pull magnets apart, or force two like poles together with your hands, not even the strength of two tug-of-war teams could pull negative electrons away from a positively charged nucleus, or force two nuclei to fuse together.

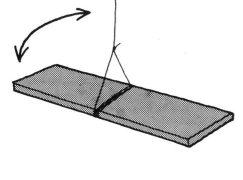

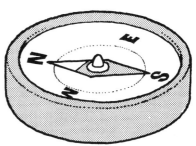

Second, to understand the problems of containing a plasma, try this experiment. Take an old wire coat hanger and reshape it into a loop with a long handle.

Then make a kind of fishing net by taping a paper bag to the frame. You can contain a certain amount of water in the bag quite easily: but what happens if you put that water into a kettle and turn it into steam? (Remember that steam can scald you so do not put your hands in it.) Holding the wire handle, try to catch the steam from the spout in the bag. Even if you hold the bag right over the spout, the steam still escapes. The problem is that heat has made the water change into a much less-easily-handled form, steam: and that is exactly what happens to the gas as it becomes plasma. Remember not to let the kettle boil dry during this experiment!

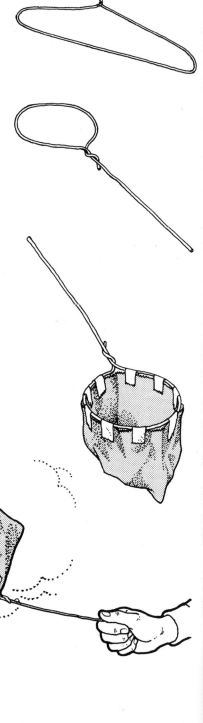

Copper-eating Bugs

Bacteria do many amazing things – besides giving us food poisoning or even more nasty diseases. They live almost everywhere – anywhere in fact where there's food to help them grow and multiply. And one unsavoury place full of good food for bacteria is sewage. So good use has been made of this fact: Cardiff scientists have deliberately grown five special kinds of bacteria found in sewage. These special bacteria between them were capable of eating copper compounds – chemicals which all too frequently can pollute water, making it dangerous for humans to use. So the scientists tried raising the bacteria in copper-polluted water, and what they hoped for actually happened. The bacteria greedily digested all the poisonous copper in the water, purifying it in the process. And what's more, they turned themselves into a kind of living copper. Forty per cent of their weight was pure copper: by smelting the bacteria in their millions, pure copper could be produced as easily as from copper ore. So, far from causing something nasty like upset stomachs, these bacteria have been made very useful to man – purifying water and producing copper at the same time.

Fishy Shoes and Handbags

Many expensive leather shoes or handbags cost a lot of money because of the skill with which they are made. But they also are expensive simply because some leathers – such as snakeskin or alligator – are rare and difficult to process. And since many reptiles are following in the footsteps of the dinosaurs, and getting nearer to extinction, other skins had to be found if traditional scaled leather was to be available at a realistic price. The Italians, traditional makers of fine leather goods, were the first to come up with an answer: fish skins.

Fortunately cod is in plentiful supply – and usually the skins are simply thrown away once the flesh has been cut out. By deep freezing the skins as soon as possible in brine the leather tanners can prevent it rotting and, with a still secret commercial process, they can stabilise the skin into a strong and beautiful leather exactly like reptile skin. So next time you go down to your local fish and chip shop, you might just hear someone order a large cod and chips – and a pair of Italian shoes!

Shooting Trees

One day you are strolling through the park, wandering between the streaks of sunlight dappling their way through the tree leaves. The peaceful calm of all this is beginning to relax you when suddenly your attention is caught by a man striding purposefully up to the slender trunk of an exotic tree. He draws a gun, presses it against the bark – and fires. You are not dreaming – this is not an episode from some bizarre thriller: he is actually helping the tree to live, not killing it.

The man would have fired a piece of dowel into the tree – a dowel impregnated with a greenish material called *Trichoderma viride*. This is a fungus, which does not harm the tree: but will attack, cover, and eventually destroy another fungus, *Condrostereum purpureum* – which is the sign of Silver-leaf disease. This *does* damage trees: fruit trees are especially vulnerable. So research scientists hit on the idea of dosing trees with the harmless fungus to kill the harmful one. But hypodermic syringes could not get through the tree bark, and so dowel bullets from a gun became the dramatic way to give the trees their life-saving injection.

Liquid Crystal Pictures

Ask someone the time, and if they say "Eighteen twenty-nine" rather than "nearly half-past six", the chances are that they are wearing a digital watch. These new ways of telling the time have become popular because of three different relatively cheap but incredibly reliable ingredients: a quartz crystal to count down the seconds: a microprocessor to direct operations and control the watch: and a liquid crystal display, or L.C.D., to show numbers on the watch face.

The L.C.D. works because of the special property of the tiny crystals involved. If a tiny electric current is applied to them, they arrange themselves differently. So, by packing in billions of them into a flat display area, and then applying an electric current to specified groups of the crystals, you can reorganise the crystals to reveal different shapes – numbers or letters or pictures. It is rather like giving thousands of spectators in a sports stadium different coloured cards to hold up. Each person knows when to display which colour, and if everyone gets it right, clever messages or pictures can be shown. You might just remember the bear which was the symbol of the Moscow Olympics. The crowd was so well organised that at the end of the games, they created a picture of the bear and made a tear run down its cheek.

To do that sort of thing with L.C.D.s is not quite so simple. You can certainly devise changes in electric currents to move the crystals: but seeing them is less easy. And they cannot display colours. This is because L.C.D.s rely on the way light is reflected back off the crystals. In one position, the crystals reflect back light in such a way that it can pass through a plastic filter above them known as a polarising filter. In another position the crystals' light is blocked by the polarising filter, and cannot get through. So those crystals make up the black area of the display, while the crystals arranged so the light gets through make up the white areas. Rearrange the crystals, and you rearrange the black and white areas of the display and so change the numbers or message.

Besides giving no choice of colours, this way of displaying the arrangements of the crystals also suffers from the fact that you need to look directly on to the L.C.D. Viewed from too much of an angle, the polarising effect of the filter cannot be seen, and the display suddenly appears much less distinct. But scientists have now discovered a rather special kind of dye, which has molecules which absorb some white light when it arrives from one direction and so reflect back a colour. But if the light arrives from another direction, the dye cannot absorb any of the light, and it is all reflected back as clear white light. Mixed in with the liquid crystals, these dye molecules are physically changed by the crystals moving when an electrical current is passed through them: so they show up as either a colour or white as required. And because the dye is right in with the crystals, there is no polarising filter, and no loss of picture when viewed from an angle.

When you remember that a colour television picture is made up by an electrical signal arranging to illuminate red, green or blue points on the screen, and that combinations of these points produce all the colours, it is not hard to imagine that soon scientists will find a way to create liquid crystal displays that show moving pictures in full colour. Imagine watching the next Olympics – all the races, not just a display of a tear rolling down a bear's cheek – on your wristwatch!

If you've ever taken a tumble on a bathroom floor, you'll be glad to know that help is on the way: there's actually a robot with the single task of measuring slipperiness. By dragging a probe behind it, it can see what resistance the tiled floor it is sent across can offer. That way the tile manufacturer can be sure that we should have less slippery tiles – and fewer accidents – in tomorrow's bathrooms, swimming pools and showers.

The smooth ceramic surface of these tiles reveals its slipperiness through the new meter.

Dialysis You Can Carry

Our kidneys play a vital role in keeping us healthy. They act as sophisticated filters, removing waste products deposited in our bloodstream during the normal processes of eating, breathing and using our bodies. If the kidneys stop working for some reason, then the waste can build up to a lethal level. So people who have damaged kidneys – say from a disease or an accident – either have to have a kidney transplant or they have to have a regular treatment called dialysis.

Dialysis means passing the blood through some sort of artificial filter in order to remove the waste. One conventional kind of kidney machine does this by using an artificial membrane. This is a special kind of cellophane, through which blood and water cannot pass. But if special chemicals are mixed in the water on one side of the membrane, they can draw the poisonous chemicals in the blood *through* the membrane. The blood is thus cleansed and allowed to circulate back around the body – and the water is simply thrown away.

Interestingly, there is a membrane in our bodies which has the same properties as the artificial membrane. It is called the peritoneal membrane: and it surrounds the intestines just below the skin to help keep them protected and comfortable. Some specially suitable dialysis patients have been able to cleanse their blood by introducing the special chemicals into a space behind this peritoneal membrane, so that they draw the poisons from the blood as it flows past the membrane on the other side, to feed the stomach muscles. The chemicals were originally inserted in hospital by trained staff using a small tube or catheter; but now a few patients are trying a system where they can attach a bag of chemicals to the catheter, which is left permanently in the body, without supervision. This means they simply hold the bag up above the catheter and let the chemicals drain out of the bag into their bodies: then they roll up the bag and keep it in a pocket or handbag for six hours, when the chemicals will need changing. The bag is simply reconnected to the tube, and left to hang below the catheter so that the chemicals drain out by gravity. A new lot of chemicals can then be put into the body and the old chemicals disposed of.

It may not sound very elegant, but it has been received enthusiastically by those dialysis patients who would otherwise need to be plugged into a kidney machine at regular intervals. They now have the freedom to go where they like, instead of always having to be within easy access of a kidney machine. But remember that the dialysis bag may not be suitable for everyone, and so do not be disappointed if your doctor tells you or a friend who needs dialysis that he cannot get one for you.

The House of the Future

If you've ever wondered what kind of home you might have in the twenty-first century, you should visit the windswept desert wastes of Arizona in the USA. Because there, more than half-buried in the sand, is Ahwatukee – the House of Shining Dreams. The sand helps to insulate its rooms, so that they are cool by day, and yet warm by night. For Ahwatukee is an energy-saving house, making full use of the hot sun during the Arizona summer, storing the energy of its warmth in several ways. While the sun heats the stretch of sand around the walls only slowly; it heats water in the pipe-

Like an iceberg, Ahwatukee shows only its tip above ground level.

Solar cells reflecting the sun from which they take energy.

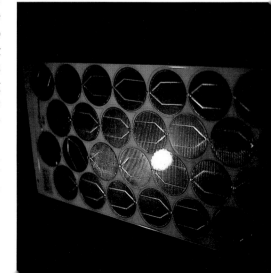

work of its towering pyramid of a roof more quickly. The water once heated is carefully stored in heavily insulated tanks until it is needed. So too is the electricity, which is generated from a whole array of solar panels to the side of the house – a significant way to cut down the fuel bills. In fact the house only uses cheap, night-time electricity for all its heating and air conditioning needs. The air conditioning, for instance, depends on a huge store of ice being made at night, and slowly allowed to melt during the day.

And you won't be caught out by a sudden freak change in the weather, because Ahwatukee has a computer to control everything that goes on within its walls. A computer which makes sure that your fuel bills are always as low as possible by constantly calculating which power source – solar panels or national electricity grid for instance – is the most economic to use for each task. And the computer does a lot, lot more. You won't even get into the house if it doesn't like you. Before the front door can be opened from the outside, you have to

When Ahwatukee's sensors discover a fire, the computer is automatically programmed to alert occupants, turn on the lights and open the doors.

No key can open Ahwatukee's door: enter your code number, and the voice synthesiser welcomes you by name and opens the door.

announce yourself to a microphone in the wall next to it. The computer analyses your voice pattern, and if it has been programmed to recognise your voice and let you in, it quite charmingly says "Welcome to Ahwatukee, John Smith". (Or whatever your name is.)

Even though Ahwatukee has no windows, there's no need to look for the light switch. Motion sensors detect just where people are in the house, and the computer automatically switches on lights for them; and of course switches them off again if you move out of any one area to another. The computer will also look after you while you sleep: with the aid of smoke detectors it will help deal with a fire for instance. The computer not only wakes up the occupants with a loud warning cry of "Fire", but also telephones the fire brigade. Nor will there be a problem with burglars. Ahwatukee can even leave the front door open to let in a cooling breeze without putting your valuables at risk. The system is designed not only to detect the temperature and prevailing wind, so as to know when to let in some free air conditioning: also it will discover if a stranger sets foot in the building, automatically call the police, and warn the occupants with an emphatic call of "Intruder in the House".

Impressed? This is only the beginning. By hooking up Ahwatukee's computer with a telephone and television, the house of the future could allow you to do even more amazing things before long. You might be able to see people on the other side of the world as you talk to them on the telephone; draw pictures with them and play computer games with them on your television screen; take a look at the shelves in your favourite shops – anywhere in the world – and place an order for the goods that you fancy; join a world-wide class of pupils studying, say, physics with the help of teachers as far apart as London, Moscow and New York. Because the very computer technology already available, as used in Ahwatukee, needs only a world network of glass-fibre cables to be built; after which it will be possible for you to live in the economic comfort of your house of the future without ever having to take a step outside it.

Computing in Ahwatukee's kitchen is just as vital as pots and pans.

The Electronic Network

All the ingredients for an extraordinary electronic world net-work already exist, and have all been seen on *Tomorrow's World*. Those glass-fibre cables, able to send thin beams of light for miles and miles at a time, can carry hundreds of electronic messages encoded in the light beams: many times more messages than our conventional wire systems which link up today's telephones. Even now there are enough telephone lines available for you to pick up the phone and talk to whoever you like almost anywhere in the world. With all the extra room

Above: *the optical fibres which can carry thousands of pieces of information, from telephone calls to television pictures, encoded in narrow beams of light.*

for other signals which optical fibres would give us, there is no reason why the present telephone network should not be extended many times further. For a start, a video camera's signal could be sent along with the sound of your voice – so the person you were calling could see your face on a television screen in front of him or her. And the electronic signals which are needed to programme and operate computers could be transmitted in the same way. So while you talked to and looked at your friend in Australia, you could also exchange information with your computers – maybe draw a plan and alter it between you, or play video chess, or work out some piece of maths homework. There are computer programmes now available which allow you to touch your television screen with your finger so that whatever shape your finger traces is left on the screen as a signal. The same signal can be transmitted to other computers and television sets right across the world – where your friend could use *his* finger to add to or alter the picture. With a system like this, there would be virtually nothing that you could not do. The whole world's population could even vote together to say what our governments should do. But before this extraordinary world becomes reality, there are a lot of practical problems to be solved. Who can afford the colossal expense of replacing all the conventional cables with fibre optics all over the world? And how much do we want to do everything from home, rather than visiting the shops, or our schools, factories and offices? It might seem an exciting idea, letting a video camera in a shop send you pictures of the goods on the shelf – but isn't it more fun to go to the supermarket yourself, to meet other people, and pick and choose what you want? Before the technology we have seen on *Tomorrow's World* brings you that kind of future, you may have to make up your mind whether you want it.

The Deadly Price of Falling in Love

There is no need to worry next time someone suggests you are a bit smelly. If they smile as they tell you, it could be that what they can smell is what makes you attractive to them. Scientists know that nearly all living creatures, from men and women to insects, attract their mates by secreting chemicals called pheromones. And what is more, scientists have now found a way to make some pheromones synthetically. But they are not using them to win themselves new girl friends or boy friends: they are finding them useful in the battle to kill pests. How? Take the tsetse fly for instance. By mixing a sterilising agent with the pheromones, the male flies can be attracted to take a dose of chemicals which will prevent them fertilising the female flies. And if the females are not fertilised, then there are no baby flies, and the population of tsetse flies which could carry disease is therefore reduced. Perhaps someone might try the same idea to make children eat school dinners!

Star Wars Camera

Remember those breathtaking attacks on the Empire's headquarters in the Death Star as Luke Skywalker and his fellow pilots swooped down between the buildings? Those kinds of scenes from "Star Wars," were shot using models and a rather special camera. A specially arranged series of lenses pick up everything that is seen through a glass prism at the end of a long tube no thicker than your finger; and as the tube is made to travel between model buildings what it is seeing is recorded on a more conventional part of the camera which could be one or two metres away from the prism. As long as the buildings are realistic enough, the result is a film which looks just like the view a pilot would get flying between skyscrapers.

The technique can of course make some marvellous sequences to thrill cinema goers; but it is also being used as a very accurate way of telling planning authorities or other interested parties exactly what a new building or whole development will look like from ground level. The camera is run along scale model streets with the new buildings in place; the resulting film shows what no model alone could do – just how the changes will appear to you and me as we walk or drive along. It is so realistic that already an accurate replica of the centre of San Francisco has been built. It is used to demonstrate several alternative ways to provide more office and hotel space. With the aid of the special films, the planners were able to compare the effects of a few new tall buildings with a wider spread of shorter new constructions; and gauge the affect of them on the city centre. Then both films were shown on television and the citizens asked to vote for the scheme they preferred. It might not seem as exciting as "Star Wars": but it was certainly a lot cheaper than building a number of multi-million dollar skyscrapers and then discovering that nobody liked them!

Something to Do

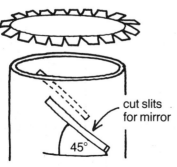

cut out circle to fit tube, with tabs to stick it down

cut slits for mirror

45°

You could try making something like the camera tube used in "Star Wars" for yourself. You will need a cardboard tube and two small mirrors.

First find, or make, the cardboard tube, about 50 or 60 centimetres long. The inside of a kitchen roll might do, but it must be just broad enough to take the two mirrors at 45° angles (see diagram). It is also worth sealing the ends of the tube with a paper cover.

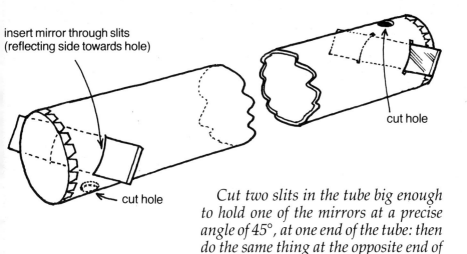

insert mirror through slits
(reflecting side towards hole)

cut hole

cut hole

Cut two slits in the tube big enough to hold one of the mirrors at a precise angle of 45°, at one end of the tube: then do the same thing at the opposite end of the tube. Then cut holes in the tube opposite each mirror.

If you have got the arrangements right, light entering the one hole will follow a path like the one shown, so that it comes in at one end of the tube and out of the other. Hold the tube so that you look in at the bottom hole – and you will see what is visible through the top hole.

Used like that, the tube is a simple periscope. You could use it to look over walls taller than yourself. But if you have a model railway layout or some other kind of model, you could try looking through the top hole and seeing your models from low down, in the same way as the planners in San Francisco did. You might even try taking a photograph through the tube's top hole – but without strong enough lights and some very good quality lenses, it would be difficult to get a good picture.

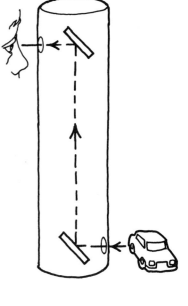

Explosive Plumbing

No one could blame you if you refused to let a plumber work on your pipes if he calmly told you he did his work with explosives. A nail put through a waterpipe with a light hammer tap is enough to flood a floor or bring down a ceiling in less than an hour; so you can imagine how devastating it would be if you blasted a hole over a centimetre in diameter into the side of a pipe. Yet our explosive plumber does exactly that, without turning the water off, whenever he wants to join a new pipe at right angles to another pipe. And he makes the new joint in a matter of seconds. It is all perfectly safe and hardly a drop of water is leaked. And it is obviously much quicker than the more traditional method of draining all the water from the pipes; cutting the old pipe all the way through, twice, to remove a section; inserting each end of the pipe into a "T" junction to make the right angle; then inserting the new pipe into the third arm of the "T" junction; and then sealing each of the three arms of the "T" into the ends of the pipe inserted into them!

The new explosive "T" junction is fitted snugly round the old pipe in exactly the position where the new pipe is to be fitted. The new pipe is fixed firmly into place at the foot of the "T". Inside the "T" junction is a hollow cutter with the explosive behind it. A hammer

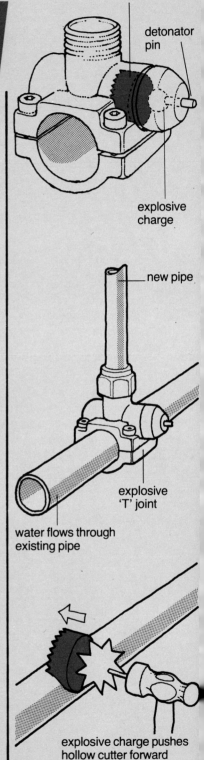

hollow cutter

detonator pin

explosive charge

new pipe

explosive 'T' joint

water flows through existing pipe

explosive charge pushes hollow cutter forward

blow is all it takes to detonate the explosive: it fires the cutter forward, making a hole in the old pipe and neatly collecting the piece cut out as it does so. Water can now rush through the hole, through the hollow cutter, and into the new pipe. The junction is complete.

Now what would be really spectacular is if someone could build something on the same lines for joining giant sewage pipes, over a metre in diameter . . .

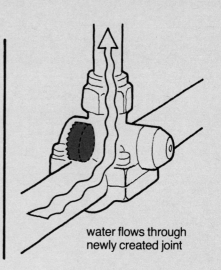

water flows through
newly created joint

Hissing Sid

It is a sad fact that often the most memorable moments on *Tomorrow's World* are when something just does not work. And perhaps most lovingly, embarrassingly remembered of all is Hissing Sid – the snooker playing, table laying, robot – who simply didn't get it right on the night.

All day long in rehearsal the compressed-air-driven arm had unfailingly potted the black on the snooker table, beating Kieran Prendiville each time. So when *Tomorrow's World* took to the air, live as usual, the special guest commentator, Ted Lowe, confidently predicted victory for the "World Champion of the Year 2000", as he dubbed Sid. But Sid did not even raise his cue. A desperate robot owner ignored all the rules and dashed on to the studio floor: tweaked a few knobs: and Sid finally took aim, much to the

73

relief of Ted Lowe and Kieran Prendiville, stumbling in unison for words to disguise this inexplicable robotic failure. Back went the cue; and just as at every rehearsal the ball slid smoothly across the table. Only this time it missed the pocket.

A rather desperate Kieran threatened Sid with one more chance – this time to arrange a place setting at a dinner table. Sid had got *that* right every time in rehearsal too. And sure enough, in his first and only live television appearance, Sid carefully and methodically proceeded to fail miserably. Cup crashed on to plate: the saucer was squeezed out sideways; so Sid produced a lot of laughs, but no evidence of his usual abilities. But there is a happy ending. There was nothing wrong with Sid's microprocessing: just a temporary shortage of the all-important compressed air. Sid works every time now.

Genetic Engineering

Imagine the convenience if tomatoes could be grown on the stalks of potato plants. Two crops would be grown in the field space of one. Or imagine the delights of doctors if inherited diseases like cystic fibrosis and haemophilia could be eliminated. Both possibilities are conceivable now because of an important new scientific technique called genetic engineering. It is as significant a development as the silicon chip, with hundreds of potential new applications – and it involves being able to control the very basic design of life itself.

All living things, from the simplest bacteria to a complex creature like you yourself, are made up of living cells. In your case, millions of them. And every living cell has the ability to reproduce itself. People grow up from babies to adults as their cells produce new and slightly changed cells continually, day in and day out. The changes go on as we age and eventually die – when the cells no longer reproduce at all. All the millions of changes throughout our lives are by no means accidental or haphazard. Every person has a unique blueprint – a plan that has been drawn up from the time he or she was conceived. This plan determines the colour of our eyes or hair for instance: and, along with other factors, it can decide when, if at all, a male will start to go bald; when his hair will turn grey; what size bust a female will have; how tall every one of us will be; maybe even how intelligent. In fact, our blueprints contain details of what makes each of us unique. And this plan is stored inside each living cell. Right inside the nucleus of every cell are tiny thread-like bodies called chromosomes. They exist in pairs: every human has twenty-two pairs of chromosomes, and two odd ones, in every cell. These chromosomes are made of a complex chemical called DNA – short for deoxyribonucleic acid. This chemical carries the details of the plan or blueprint, each tiny piece of which is called a gene. There are genes to decide eye colour, others to decide hair colour, and so on. If a living cell happens to be part of the eye, it will make active use of the eye colour gene; if the cell is part of, say the ear, it will ignore that part of the blueprint. So in each cell there is a complete string of genes even if it only "uses" a few of those genes. And that string of genes is rather like a string of numbers – basically variations in the arrangements you can make with four different numbers. So one person's genetic code might look something like 22134211134421243341 . . . while another looks something like 2122344413214332122 . . . And this is where the amazing new technique called genetic engineering comes in.

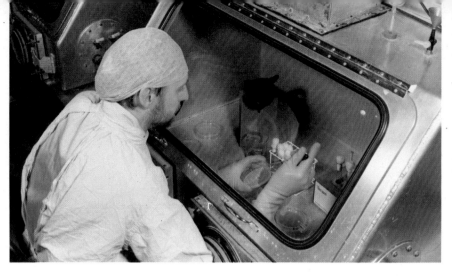

A genetic engineer in the complex sterile laboratory conditions his work demands.

Even though every living cell is microscopic in size, and the chromosomes are smaller still, so that the genes on them are so tiny that you would not believe that they could be sorted out and identified, scientists have now developed such sophisticated techniques that they can identify many precise details of the genes. For instance, they might demonstrate that there are five digits in all genetic codes on one particular chromosome, and its twin, to determine the way in which our blood clots when we cut ourselves. And since the chromosomes are in pairs, they may be able to discover that when, say, the digits 1 and 2, as the first digits of the five, on one chromosome are paired with, say, 3 and 4 on its partner, it produces a problem: the blood does not clot. Literally hundreds of thousands of number combinations would be fine – such as these pairs:

a) (12433/ . . .   b) (43122/ . . .   c) (22143/ . . .
   (33122/ . . .   (41333/ . . .   (41122/ . . .
and so on

But this pair: d) (12134/ . . .
             (43314/ . . .

has the fatal combination of genes leading to a failure of blood to clot – the disease haemophilia.

Genetic engineering is the name given to a range of techniques by which scientists can actually manipulate those number codes. As they learn more and more about our genes and how to control them, it looks as though it will only be a matter of time before they can manipulate the numbers in the haemophilia-causing genes, so that the problem disappears. In the same way they might manipulate the genes of potatoes and tomato plants, so that a hybrid plant is produced to have potato roots and tomato fruits.

It takes tremendous skill and ingenuity to do the actual manipulation or genetic engineering. Scientists use two kinds of living tools to help them: bacteria and living chemicals called enzymes.

Manufacturing companies have sprung up all over the world to exploit this new living technology which many scientists confidently predict will be as far reaching in impact as the microprocessor.

Drugs from Bugs

It is one thing to know the detailed arrangement of genes on a chromosome; but finding a way to move them or replace them or even just copy them is quite another. The genes are so microscopically small, it is almost impossible to make a surgical instrument delicate enough to cut between them and separate them out. Even more miraculous would be an instrument for assembling or manufacturing genes. But without some way of doing both jobs, no real genetic engineering can begin.

One answer to these problems is to look at nature itself. In the

Magnified 55,500 times, the genetic engineer's favourite bacteria, E. Coli, spew forth strands of genetic material.

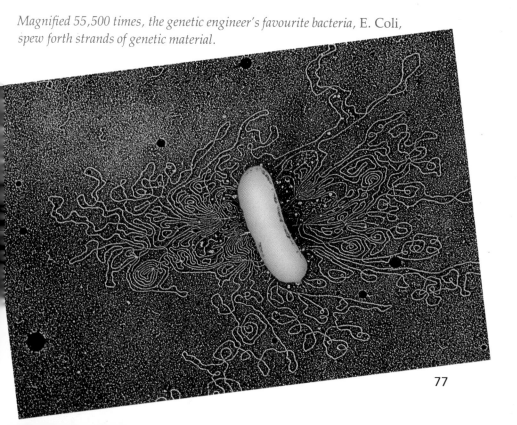

natural evolution of the living cell, DNA has to be cut into pieces by special chemicals known as enzymes. So rather than use surgical instruments to cut and prepare the various genes and chromosomes for genetic engineering, why not harness the power of the enzymes? After careful laboratory research, that is exactly how scientists have now been able to select the pieces of genetic material which most interest them. And some of those pieces do invaluable work.

Drugs, such as insulin, to help treat diabetics, and interferon, invaluable in the fight against several diseases, including cancer, are made naturally in our bodies. But these drugs are very hard to make either synthetically or by extraction from human or animal bodies. So they have always been extremely expensive and in short supply. It has meant that everything, from the regular treatment of patients to experimental research, has had to be very limited, and the full potential of the drugs has not been exploited. Until recently, that is, when the genes responsible for producing the drugs in our bodies were identified. And using enzymes it was possible to cut out the relevant pieces of DNA.

Just like that, of course, the pieces of DNA were almost useless. Any blueprint or plan can only be made use of if there is a workshop or factory in which manufacturing can take place. So a natural workshop was found to house the drug producing genes – bacteria. These tiny living crea-

OH NO!!!.. YOU'VE JUST SWATTED EIGHT THOUSAND POUNDS WORTH OF INSULIN !

tures are simple enough in their structure to accept the new DNA and follow its instructions; so that a bug full of insulin could be created by carefully manipulating insulin producing genes into it. Similarly, an interferon bug could be developed.

After that, nature really does do the rest. Because when drug-producing bacteria breed, they give birth to more drug-producing bacteria. And in a favourable environment, with warmth and food to encourage them, each of the bacteria divides into two, then those two divide again making four, then eight, then sixteen, then thirty-two . . . until very quickly there are millions of them. Millions of bacteria containing a pure form of a valuable drug. Once the colony has started, it can go on growing indefinitely; and so the majority of the bacteria can be "harvested" at regular intervals, then killed, and the drugs purified out.

Genetically-engineered insulin and interferon have now been produced successfully this way, and will soon be commonplace on chemists' shelves. And the power of the drug bugs is only beginning to be explored. There are literally hundreds of materials produced in the body which could now be artificially "farmed" in the same way as insulin. It means that once we know the body's way of dealing with problems, we may well be able to mimic the process that produces a cure for today's incurable diseases — simply by breeding genetically-engineered bacteria.

However valuable it is, producing drugs from bacteria using genetic engineering is only the beginning. There are plenty of other ways in which scientists can engineer genes; and one basic tool for their work is the gene machine. This is simply a rather special box in which pieces of DNA can be built up, gene by gene, in order to mimic natural genes. At first sight the box does a very simple job; it simply adds one chemical after the next into a long chain. But because it is all being done at such microscopic levels, it takes some extremely clever arranging.

The DNA and its genes are built up from the four basic chemicals described in *Genetic Engineering* (page 75) – we will call them 1, 2, 3 and 4. So a typical piece of natural DNA might look like this:

211344121133432 . . .

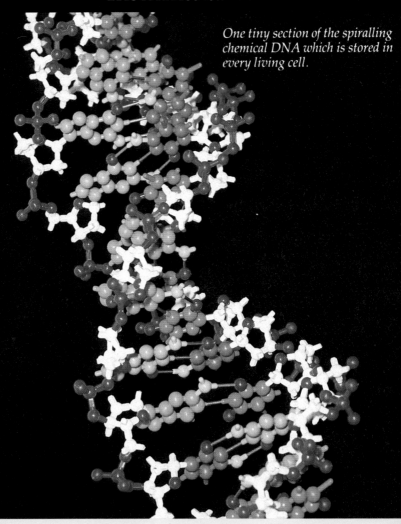

One tiny section of the spiralling chemical DNA which is stored in every living cell.

Clearly, if we want to make a copy of that DNA from basic chemicals, we have to start with 2, then add chemical 1, twice, then 3, then 4 and so on.

The gene machine provides a way to do this. It relies on the fact that a molecule of each of the four chemicals is rather like a jigsaw piece, with a different kind of shape at either end:

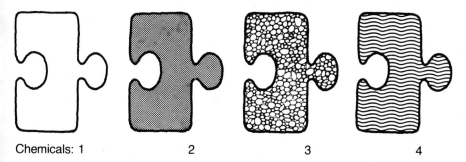

Chemicals: 1   2   3   4

You can see that any of the chemicals can easily be connected to any of the other chemicals – or itself. But how can you handle the chemicals one molecule at a time, to make a precise sequence for a DNA chain?

The clever technique involved requires a fifth chemical. It is, if you like, a different jigsaw piece: it fits on to one end of one molecule of any of the other four chemicals – but it cannot then fit on to the other end of another molecule. Effectively it "blocks" the connecting end of the other chemical molecules to prevent them joining up.

Chemical 5

With all five chemicals ready to hand, it is now possible to use the gene machine. Basically it consists of a container in which there is an "anchor point" on to which a molecule of any of the chemicals will fit. (This anchor is in fact just another chemical with the right jigsaw end to fit into any of the other chemicals.)

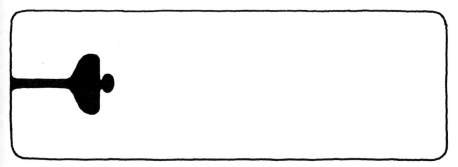

If we want to build the DNA sequence 211344121133432 . . ., the first step is to take some of the chemical 2. Even in a small amount, there will be thousands of molecules. You mix this 2 with so much of the chemical number 5, that every single molecule of 2 will be "blocked" by joining up with a molecule of 5:

Any "spare" molecules of 5 will be then removed from the mixture, chemically, so that it is entirely made up of the "blocked" molecules of 2.

This whole mixture is then poured into the gene machine container. Just one of the blocked molecules will attach itself to the anchor:

Chemicals 2 and 5

All the other molecules cannot join up, because they are blocked. So they can be flushed out of the container, leaving just the one molecule attached to the anchor.

Next the container is flooded with chemicals which will simply remove the molecule of chemical 5 from the molecule of chemical 2. When the container is flushed out, one molecule of "unblocked" chemical 2 is left anchored in the container.

The next chemical in the chain is 1. So a mixture of chemical 1 and chemical 5 is prepared, in order to produce a number of "blocked" molecules of chemical 1:

Now every step of the procedure is repeated.

Chemicals 1 and 5

1. The "blocked" molecules of 1 are put into the container; so only one will join on to the anchored molecule of 2.

2. The "blocked" molecules of 1 are flushed out.

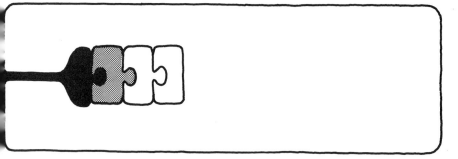

3. The molecule of 1 plus 5 is chemically "unblocked".

Now the process is repeated with a second molecule of 1. The next molecule in the chain is a 3, then a molecule of 4 is added, then a second molecule of 4, then a 1, then 2, then 1, then 1 again . . . and so the chain is built up molecule by molecule to the exact requirements. It means that scientists can artificially create any DNA sequence they like. One day they may be able to make "good" sequences of DNA to replace "bad". Take the case of haemophilia for example. In theory, doctors could soon take a human egg, fertilised in the laboratory, and while it was still only a single cell, the "bad" DNA sequences causing the disease could be identified, cut out from the chromosomes, using enzymes, and replaced with "good" sequences artificially made in the gene machine. The single cell would then be implanted into the mother's womb, just like any other test-tube baby. There it would divide into two, then four, cells and go on to develop in the normal way – except that the slightly altered genetic code would not produce haemophilia in the child when it was born. Scientists could treat cystic fibrosis and other inherited diseases in the same way – just as soon as they get a complete picture of all the genes on all the chromosomes, and learn what they control.

The trouble is that when they know that, they will also know how to manipulate intelligence or eye colour or any of our characteristics. And that means we could soon build people to order. Parents of the future could choose their children by number, to be a specific height, with planned skills and a selected hair and eye colour. No surprises. Assembly line people like assembly line cars – we could soon come to accept the fashion of the day in ordering our children. If you do not like that idea, then you must think fast how best we should control the work going on with bacteria and gene machines, so that it is used only to produce valuable drugs and prevent diseases: not to control our personalities.

The Computer Doctor

When you go to your doctor, it is important to answer his questions as honestly and accurately as possible. It is largely from what you say that he decides how to treat you. Once he recognises your symptoms, and how seriously you are affected, he can select the right medicines, and tell you how often to take them. But it is not always easy for patients to be as honest and straightforward with the doctor as they should. Sometimes it is embarrassing to talk about things that bother us to another person. And so in some cases doctors are finding that they can help their patients more by letting them discuss their symptoms with a computer!

The computer is programmed to ask the patient questions by displaying them on a television screen; and the patient types in answers with a standard typewriter keyboard. The answer to the first question determines what the computer asks next: and when it has enough information from the patient it can offer a prescription. Patients sometimes find that they can answer those embarrassing questions much more easily when all they are talking to is a load of electronic circuitry. And the real doctors can of course monitor the computer's results to make sure that it is doing a good job!

The Latest Light Bulbs

Light bulbs are vital to us in the twentieth century. Imagine what would happen if they all failed at once. Millions of people would be helpless, unable to see to cook and work or play after dark. Yet surprisingly the light bulb is a fairly crude piece of technology that has hardly changed since it was first invented by Joseph Swann and Thomas Edison about a hundred years ago. Electricity heats a wire inside a glass bulb until it glows with heat to give light. But the wire is very frail and

The new fluorescent bulbs may bear little resemblance to conventional light bulbs.

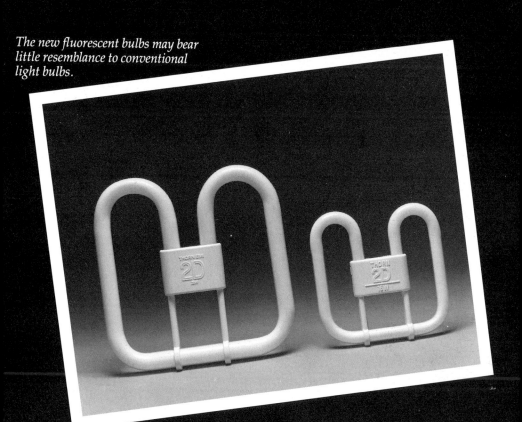

eventually breaks, worn brittle by repeated heating and cooling. Fluorescent tubes last much longer than standard light bulbs: there is no wire to break because inside the tube is a gas which the electricity excites to produce ultra-violet light. This in turn becomes visible light when it hits phosphorus on the side of the tube. But fluorescent tubes will not fit into the traditional electrical fittings in millions of homes all over the world. So most of us still have to put up with normal short-lived light bulbs.

But not for long. The shortest viable fluorescent tube is about twenty-three centimetres long – stretched out straight. With the blinding flash of inspiration that leads people to an obvious solution, one large lighting manufacturer hit on the amazing idea of bending the tube, and packing it inside a standard light bulb. The first design for the new bulb was rather heavy for many light fittings – and it cost forty times as much as an ordinary bulb. But then it lasts longer and costs 75% less to run. So not surprisingly, new designs are being tried to make the fluorescent bulb lighter and cheaper. If they succeed, we might all one day be grateful to the man who first thought of bending the fluorescent tube.

Silence in the Cockpit

The thrilling aerobatic displays performed by the Red Arrows demand split-second timing and total concentration from the pilots, and if you find the noise deafening as they roar over your head into a breathtaking formation – think what it must be like for the pilots. It is amazing they can concentrate at all, let alone hear each other's messages from the tiny loudspeakers fitted inside their helmets. But there is an ingenious way now to help reduce all that noise – and it actually means feeding *more* noise into the pilot's helmet in order to make *less*!

The principle seems a lot less contradictory if you consider that you can make a hot drink cooler by adding more of the same drink – which is much colder. When the liquids mix the two opposite temperatures cancel each other out, and you are left with a drink which is just the right temperature. In the same way you can mix a noise which is exactly opposite to another noise and produce a mixture of noise which is just right – in other words, virtual quietness. If silence is given a number value 0, then a sound valued at 10 can be reduced to silence by adding a sound of -10 to it.

The new system does this by reading all the sound in the cockpit through a microphone, and constantly feeding that sound to an original electronics device. The wave form – if you like, the number values – of that sound is noted; and instantly a sound is created with the opposite waveform. This is then fed back into the pilot's helmet where a loudspeaker plays it into his ear along with the regular noise of the cockpit. The two sounds cancel each other out: and the pilot hears almost nothing. Except of course when another loudspeaker in the helmet feeds him a message over the radio communications system from the pilots of other aircraft in the formation; and without distraction from other sounds they can soar in unison to fly with wing tips seemingly touching before spreading out and swooping down to reform again.

The team work of the Red Arrows which owes so much to clear commands and instant response.

Music from Any Old Sound

Nowadays you can find people making music from the most unlikely sounds. You may have heard a chorus of lamb bleats giving a weird version of "Baa Baa Black Sheep", or a dog-barks version of "How Much Is That Doggy In The Window?" on record request programmes. They are the light-hearted evidence of a whole new dimension in music making, combining the skills of computing with the electronic synthesiser and digital recording.

Sound is transmitted as waves travelling through the air; and every different sound makes a different wave form or pattern. You have probably seen a typical wave form on an oscilloscope, a special device to show the "shape" of a sound wave.

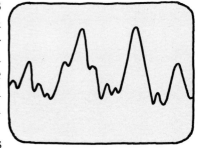

A typical wave form.

Traditionally, recording sounds involved copying that wave form as an electrical signal, as accurately as possible on to a magnetic tape, and then converting it back into sound later on, on a tape recorder for instance. It was really quite limited as people could only reproduce sounds that were actually made in front of a microphone, and only reproduce them as accurately as the magnetic copy would allow. Magnetic tape is in fact a coating of magnetic particles on a roll of plastic tape; and there are tiny spaces between the particles. So a sound with a wave form like diagram A might record a copy rather like diagram B. The reproduction of the sound can only "guess" at what the gaps should be, and so the recording cannot be "as good" as the original sound.

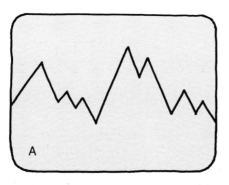

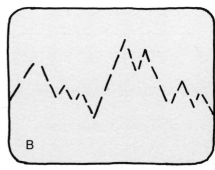

Digital recording makes it possible to reproduce sound much more accurately. Instead of copying the wave form on to tape, it is described as a long number code, which is recorded. Every single point on the wave form is given numbers, a bit like giving a map reference using a grid. In the diagram of the wave form, for instance, point A would be on line 3 of the vertical scale and line 1.5, half-way between 1 and 2, on the horizontal scale. Point B would be at 10 and 7. And so on.

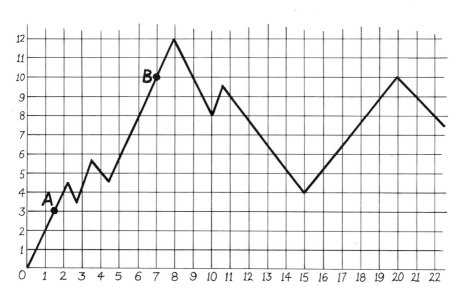

How a wave form might appear on a grid.

If you were to write out all the numbers that refer to each point on the wave form one after another, you would have a number, or *digital*, code for the sound. Numbers, of course, are

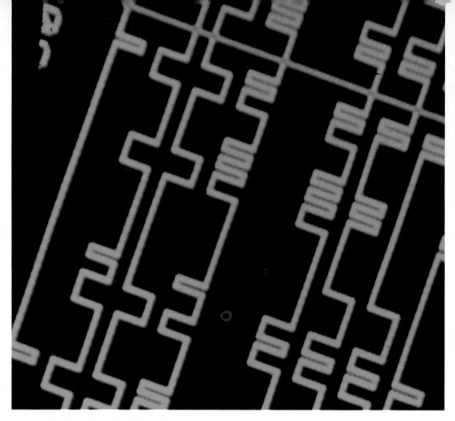

Digital pulses displayed on a screen.

no problem for a computer. It can read literally millions of them in a fraction of a second. So in no time at all, the digital code number for a single sound can be calculated and memorised. What is more, the computer can soon use mathematical formulae to calculate the code for "exactly the same sound, one octave higher". In this way, all the notes of the musical scale can be reproduced; and with that basic information, the computer can be programmed to write tunes, change key – in fact, make any musical arrangement you like. In other words, you can record any old sound, identify its wave form, and the computer will do the rest. It can speedily calculate all the notes for Beethoven's Fifth Symphony, using only the sound of one breaking milk bottle as a source for all the music! This is what is called synthesising – producing music without instruments, electronically, by computing all the notes based on the digital code for a single sound. That sound can of course be a top quality violin, piano or oboe – so the whole orchestra can be synthesised from recordings of single notes from each instrument. But somehow it is hard to imagine all those colourful promenaders singing "Land of Hope and Glory" to the accompaniment of a computer – so musicians need not give up – just yet!

Sailing by Satellite

S ailors lost on the world's angry seas have something to thank the space programme for. Because now those sailors have a new way to find out where they are – using satellites orbiting high above the earth. Some of these flying watchdogs are continually transmitting information back to the earth which helps to identify the exact spot on the earth's surface where the receiver picks up their signals. So a sailor trying to find his way only needs a special receiver and a microprocessor to pinpoint his position. The microprocessor is needed to translate the satellites' messages and give a longitude and latitude reading. It's so accurate that you can work out where you are, anywhere in the world, within a mere hundred metres or so. The satellites were originally put up to help guide Polaris submarines – but now anyone can have access to their signals, and several manufacturers are making satellite navigation receivers for you to plug into any boat you want.

Memory Metal

Springs are wonderful things. Press them flat, twist them, bend them about in all directions – and they always return to the same size and shape that they started. Or at least they used to. Because you can now get springs which have different sizes and shapes – according to how hot or cold they are. The secret is in the way the metal is manufactured; because it can be made to "remember" one length at one temperature, and another length at a totally different temperature. This special metal does a lot more than expand normally by tiny amounts when it is heated, instead the actual atoms restructure themselves as the temperature changes. Stresses between the thousands of atoms which make up each crystal of metal force the crystals to realign quite dramatically. The sensitivity of the metal makes it an ideal potential thermostat. It has already been used in springs which contract with the cold and expand when it gets warmer to open and close greenhouse windows to match changes in the weather.

And, more recently, an ingenious kind of motor has been developed. A loop of wire made from the metal, and run around two pulley wheels, can be used to turn them – simply by heating the wire at one point. As it changes shape in the heat, the wire pushes the wheels around, moving itself along in the process. So a new section of wire arrives to be heated – in turn pushing the wheels further round. And so on. As long as part of the wire is heated, and the rest of it cooled when out of the heat source, the wheels will keep turning. The potential for using otherwise wasted heat is enormous – a car's exhaust could be used to turn the wire loop for instance, providing energy to help drive the fan belt. There is clearly a bright future for this metal that knows the difference between hot and cold.

Earthworm Omelette

Believe it or not, one of the richest sources of protein you could find is the common earthworm, which you can dig up in any garden. Because it consists of a long wall of muscle, which it uses to make its way through the soil, and a simple digestive system, the worm is 60% to 70% pure protein. Very nutritious. But do not rush out to eat one – just yet. Because you have to have them thoroughly cleaned and, to put it politely, evacuated, so that you don't spoil that special worm taste with any other flavours from the soil – or even the sewage – on which worms thrive. In fact worms are being seriously cultivated in sewage to provide protein for animal feed on the farm. And anything animals can eat safely – by and large – so can we. So here is a recipe for "Omelette aux vers de terre" – earthworm omelette, in other words.

First collect and clean your worms, then leave them to evacuate in a sterile environment where they cannot find food. This takes about three hours. Then clean and freeze the worms, until required for cooking. Freeze-dry them and powder them if you like – that is what the animal feed manufacturers are doing. After that, you simply mix the eggs for an omelette, stir in the worms, and fry in the usual way. The taste is hardly anything special, but certainly not objectionable. But do not be surprised if your Mum is not exactly keen to let you find out for yourself!

People working on oil rigs in the North Sea have to travel back and forth to the mainland time and time again by helicopter. And it is about as uneventful for them as taking a bus to work. But in the interests of safety, they are often trained for at least one dramatic emergency – when the pilot is forced to land the helicopter in the sea. Dramatic, because in only slightly rough weather the helicopter is likely to capsize and sink. In order to survive, the passengers and crew need to keep calm and follow a strict escape procedure so they can swim to the surface to be rescued. The difficulty of practising is obvious – you can hardly crash land and sink helicopters regularly to get the escape routine right! So at Robert Gordon's Institute of Technology in Aberdeen they have made an extraordinary emergency trainer. It looks rather like a huge baked beans tin; in fact it is a realistic replica of the cabin section of a helicopter. It is held firmly in place over a huge tank of water, the size of a small swimming pool. But it is kept secure by a compressed air brake which can only be released when the passengers and crew are inside. A winch lowers the cylinder into the water – and it is so designed that it can revolve freely once the brake is off.

Training in case of disaster. Divers are on hand to help any trainees who get into difficulties.

Buoyancy chambers below the floor of the cylinder make sure that it turns over, rapidly dumping the occupied part of the cylinder under water. The passengers then follow the routine they have tried several times on dry land and can escape comfortably and surface. The advantage of a controlled situation like this is that underwater experts can be on hand to help the people being trained if they get into difficulties.

Nylon Nails

What do you think would happen if you hammered three nails into a block of wood, and then tried to plane it and sandpaper it down to half its thickness? No prizes for those who do carpentry and come up with the obvious answers – a blunted and dented blade in your plane, and shredded sandpaper. Nails are terrific for holding wood together, but not a lot of fun when you forget they are there and want to smooth the wood down.

Now for a question where the right answer *is* worth a prize: what would happen if you loaded a shotgun with a candle, and fired it at a strong wooden door? No prizes for anyone who says the candle would end up as a flattened blob of wax stuck to the door: because, believe it or not, fired at a high enough speed, something as soft as a wax candle can go right through a much harder substance such as wood.

Which brings us back to nails. If you made a nail soft enough to be planed or sandpapered, you could save an awful lot of plane blades and sandpaper. All you would need is something to fire them fast enough into the wood. A shotgun is not exactly standard equipment for a carpenter, so a gun working with compressed air is a better bet. With it, you can fire nails made of nylon into wood instead of hammering in those tool-wrecking wire ones. The nylon is just as strong as the metal nails, once securely in place.

By the way, if you were thinking of trying to fire a candle through a door – please, don't! It takes an expert to do it correctly and safely: the candle *can* get stuck in the gun barrel, sealing it, and causing the explosive force of the gun shot to split the gun barrel apart. But it really has been done – as regular viewers of *Tomorrow's World* have seen.

Helping People Have Babies

One of the most amazing advances in science recently has been the progress that has been made to help men and women who are having problems in starting a family for one reason or another. Within two weeks in 1980 Tomorrow's World was the first to report two significant advances. One was a development of "test tube baby" research; but first was a timely reminder that this is not the only way to help mothers who have pregnancy difficulties.

Suzanne and Tony Smith had wanted a baby desperately for five years; but although Suzanne became pregnant four times, she always went into labour and gave birth before the baby had properly developed, so it could not survive. So doctors tried an experiment with a drug called sabutomol which is normally given to help relax the breathing of asthma patients. A mechanical pump was linked to one of Suzanne's veins when she became pregnant a fifth time – and it supplied a regular low dose of sabutomol to her body. And it did the trick. This time she did not go into labour early, and gave birth to a fine healthy baby.

Only a week later, we announced that the Royal Free Hospital had taken test tube baby techniques one step further on. Some women find that they cannot produce eggs, so that they can never conceive a baby naturally in their own bodies. What the Royal Free Hospital did was to help these women have babies from an egg donated by another woman which had been fertilised by the patient's husband's sperm in the laboratory.

The eggs have to be removed at exactly the right time from the donor: ultrasound scans are used to observe the egg production to pinpoint this exactly. The egg is carefully and painlessly drawn out by suction down a long slender tube inserted through the abdomen. The egg is then checked under a microscope before being added to a small glass container in which the father's sperm is carefully diluted. After twelve hours, one sperm will have fertilised the egg, creating a living cell: by twenty-four hours, this will divide into two cells, and by forty-eight hours it will have become four cells. Then, at the eight-cell stage, seventy-two hours after the sperm and egg were first introduced, the tiny collection of living cells is carefully floated in liquid, and inserted, down a very fine tube, into the patient.

Doctors and scientists are now beginning to untangle all the problems which these new skills bring. They are all fairly clear, for instance, that there can be nothing morally wrong in helping women like Suzanne Smith have her baby. The baby was

With the aid of microscopic photography, the start of a new life: the magical moment when a sperm penetrates and fertilises a female egg.

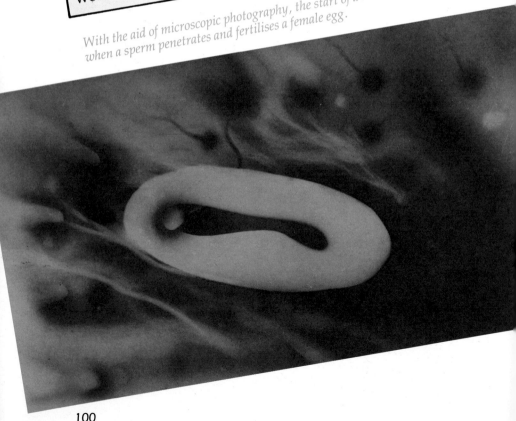

100

The first of the so-called test-tube babies; Louise Brown, whose life began with the fertilisation of an egg in the laboratory.

conceived and allowed to develop naturally; only the premature labour was controlled artificially. Many people would argue that letting a baby develop outside the mother's body is also acceptable, so long as there is no interference with the natural progress of the development of the cells. But there are now techniques for storing these early embryos by freezing them, then later unfreezing them to allow them to develop naturally. Scientists in Cambridge have even taken an embyro lamb at the four-cell stage, and split it into two separate two-cell embyros. One was frozen: the other was transplanted back into its mother. The frozen one was unfrozen two months later, and then transplanted into another sheep. Both sheep gave birth to perfectly healthy lambs – identical twins artificially made from the same fertilised egg, but born two months apart. No scientists have yet admitted to such experiments with human embryos, and many people would be horrified if they did. Although it is wonderful that we have the scientific skill to help mothers who have had problems conceiving and carrying healthy babies, it is also enormously difficult to decide where our experiments with life should be allowed to take us.

A small version of the OTEC system.

Energy from the Sea

Whenever you feel the wind on your cheek or try to swim against the power of the waves at the seaside, you are experiencing the kind of energy that exists naturally in the world all around us. But it is not easy to harness such energy to meet our needs. Winds can power ships by filling their sails – but there is no guarantee that they will blow when you want them. And in our busy world, industry cannot afford to be at the mercy of a change in the weather. Electricity, constantly available, has become the kind of power we now rely on: and converting natural energy to electricity remains a fascinating challenge.

Electricity is simply a stream of sub-atomic particles called electrons. There are various ways to create such a stream of particles, and to use their power. The electrons are a bit like water in a sponge: just as water could be wrung out of a huge sponge and sent down a pipe to a tap, from which the water could be released and used, so a stream of electrons can be separated from atoms and made to travel along a wire to a switch, where it can be released and used. A stream of electrons is created for instance in a wire coil, which moves around a magnet: and most electricity generators keep a coil turning around a magnet one way or another. Windmills can be made to turn the coil directly, as can special devices floating in the sea and harnessing the force of the waves. But so far they are not as cheap and effective as using a nuclear reactor or burning oil or coal to power a steam-driven turbine which turns the coil. The steam as it rises pushes one blade forward – another takes its place – and so on. This turns the wheel which then turns the coil.

Another, rather more unusual, attempt has been made to try to trap natural energy and make electricity. It is called OTEC, or Oceanic Thermal Energy Collection. The idea relies on the fact that heat from the sun makes the surface of the sea several degrees warmer than water below the surface, When the warm surface water reaches a temperature of eight degrees centigrade, it is warm enough to evaporate ammonia. The ammonia vapour passes through a turbine which, just like a conventional steam turbine, turns a coil to generate electricity. The vapour is then piped to deeper cooler waters where it turns back to liquid: it is then brought back to the surface, turned into vapour again – and the cycle continues. This system was used to generate 50 kilowatts of electricity when the American government tested a prototype off Hawaii. But there is still a lot of testing to be done, and costs have to be worked out before we will know if OTEC is a useful way to harness natural energy.

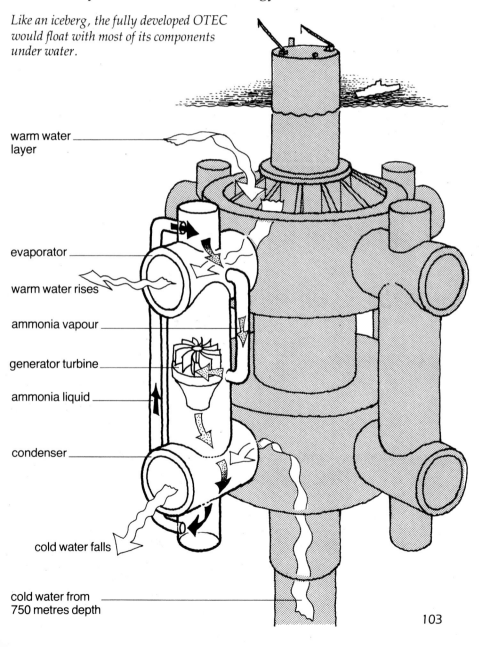

Like an iceberg, the fully developed OTEC would float with most of its components under water.

warm water layer

evaporator

warm water rises

ammonia vapour

generator turbine

ammonia liquid

condenser

cold water falls

cold water from 750 metres depth

103

Monoclonal Antibodies – the Doctor's New Friend

When you are ill, your body has a marvellous system to deal with the cause of your disease. It can produce special living cells with only one job: to annihilate foreign bodies. These cells are called antibodies and they will attach themselves to the viruses or other source of infection that we want to be rid of. The antibodies prevent the invading matter from growing and feeding on our tissue, and so eventually it dies. And better still, the antibodies, once created, leave instructions for new antibodies to be produced instantly if ever needed again; so that if the disease reappears, it can be dealt with before it has even affected us. That is how we become immune to various diseases. Inoculations involve putting a weak virus into our bodies in order to stimulate the production of antibodies, which prevent us being harmed by the stronger disease virus if it ever attacks us.

But sometimes our bodies cannot produce antibodies fast

Disease-fighting antibodies in the blood as seen through the microscope.

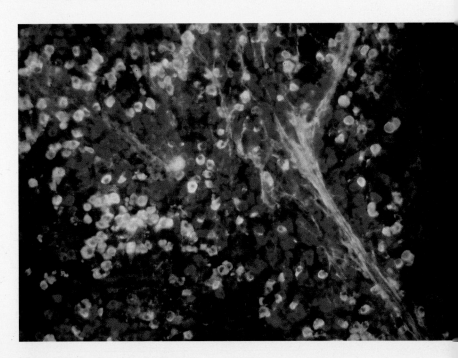

The microscopic living cells which are used to make monoclonal antibodies are delicately sorted and cultivated in the laboratory.

enough to cope with a disease. The disease virus reproduces too fast, and we become seriously ill or may even die. Doctors have tried all sorts of treatments to deal with such situations; but often the only really effective treatment would be to give the patient a dose of extra antibodies. The problem is that it is very hard to create or store antibodies, which, like many living cells, only survive well in a living body.

It is possible to cultivate antibodies in a laboratory and keep them alive briefly for just a few weeks – but a recent discovery may solve this problem. At the Molecular Biology Unit at Cambridge University, Dr César Milstein, hit upon a way to produce useful antibodies cheaply, and keep them alive outside the human body. And to do so he found a good use for cancer cells.

First of all, he took normal antibody-producing cells, that cannot survive for long outside the body. Then he mixed with them some cancer cells, which would easily reproduce themselves and survive in the laboratory. With the aid of a virus, which he added to the mixture, he caused the antibodies and the cancer cells to join together to produce a totally new kind of cell, a hybrid with the advantages of both its component cells. The new cells could multiply rapidly, survive outside the body, and have all the disease-fighting properties of the antibodies. In effect he had created a biological factory, capable of making vast quantities of exact copies of the one antibody originally joined to the cancer cell.

Antibodies made this way are called monoclonal antibodies – a technical name which simply means they are exact copies of one original antibody. They are very important to doctors because it means that for the first time we should be able to produce drugs which we know will work against common diseases like 'flu. And we should also be able to deal with some of the most serious diseases, such as hepatitis, which have been so difficult to control in the past. It just depends on whether the scientists can isolate and identify the antibodies for each disease; then make them into successful hybrids with cancer cells; and so produce effective health-giving monoclonal antibodies.

Learning about Cancer

One of the diseases which doctors would dearly love to understand better is cancer. Cancer cells are living cells which grow and reproduce uncontrollably, in the end taking over from healthy living cells, weakening and sometimes eventually killing a patient with the disease. We are learning more and more all the time about treating cancer; and many people who get various kinds of cancer do not die from it. But it remains in many ways a mystery how cancer is caused. We know that some chemicals cause cancer; even too much exposure to sunshine can cause it; so it seems does too much stress, some viruses, and even certain foods. They all appear to have nothing in common: so what is really going on?

Scientists now think they are closer to explaining all these seemingly unrelatable causes of cancer because of growth-causing genes which they have called oncogenes. (Genes, and Genetic Engineering, are described on pages 75–77.)

Oncogenes were first discovered in the DNA of viruses which were known to cause cancer in other animals, even if they did not cause cancer in humans. The scientists reasoned that if these genes were somehow transferred from the virus to an animal, they could perhaps give the instruction for living cells to "reproduce continually". And this could be how cancer was triggered. But the next steps in their research showed something they had not expected. First of all, they discovered the oncogenes in human cancer cells – and then, to their astonishment, they found the genes in every single healthy living cell in the human body!

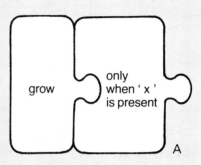

Gene message A ensures normal growth, but combination B could cause cancer.

So why are not all of our cells cancerous? It seems that oncogenes by themselves are only half of the story. Suppose each living

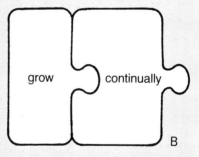

cell has these genes linked to other genes, to qualify the oncogenes' instructions. The oncogenes could be ordering "reproduce continually" while the next genes could be adding "only when hormone 'x' is present" or "only when chemical 'y' is produced". In other words, if hormone "x" or chemical "y" is only added to the living cells when they are required to reproduce in order to replace themselves – the oncogenes will then effectively only trigger natural healthy replacement of cells. But if, through some muddle, the oncogenes became connected to an instruction which said "whatever else is present", then they would be making living cells reproduce nonstop – which is exactly what cancer cells do. And what the scientists believe is the common link between many of those

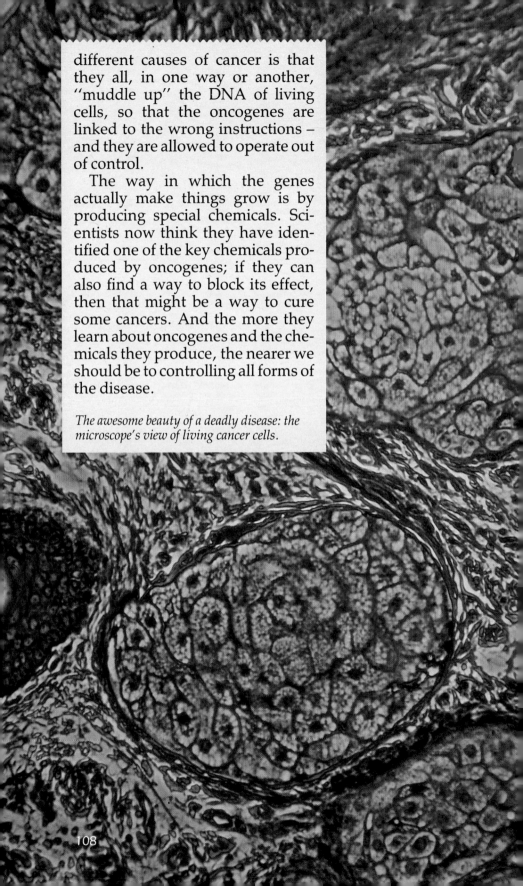

different causes of cancer is that they all, in one way or another, "muddle up" the DNA of living cells, so that the oncogenes are linked to the wrong instructions – and they are allowed to operate out of control.

The way in which the genes actually make things grow is by producing special chemicals. Scientists now think they have identified one of the key chemicals produced by oncogenes; if they can also find a way to block its effect, then that might be a way to cure some cancers. And the more they learn about oncogenes and the chemicals they produce, the nearer we should be to controlling all forms of the disease.

The awesome beauty of a deadly disease: the microscope's view of living cancer cells.

Slippers for Horses

In the early days of broadcasting two half coconut shells produced one of the most well-known sound effects for radio plays: the sound of horses' hooves clip-clopping over old-fashioned streets. Nowadays the coconut shells are rarely used: it is simpler for a tape recording of the true sound to be played into the production instead. And while the coconut shells have become obsolete – so too have the horseshoes. The motor car has taken over so many of the horse's functions, that traditional blacksmiths are no longer found in every village, so shoeing the horses that remain had to be brought into the twentieth century. The iron and nails of the traditional lucky horseshoe have given way to a plastic glove-like slipper with soft stretchy

I WARNED YOU ABOUT USING TOO MUCH SUPER GLUE!

uppers to slip over the hoof, and a hard polyurethane sole made of the plastic used for furniture castors. And the whole lot is kept firmly in place with a few dabs of super glue. Now I wonder what that lot would sound like on cobblestones?

The security services in most countries go to a lot of trouble to ensure that criminals or other undesirable people cannot easily enter the country. At every seaport and airport, immigration officers check the passports of anyone arriving from a foreign country: they try to ensure that none of them is a forgery.

It is really quite difficult to make an entirely false passport from scratch. The special kinds of paper used and the detailed patterns on them are complicated to copy. Much easier – although still very hard – is to change a stolen passport. You need to remove the photograph and substitute one of the false owner: and most important of all, you need to alter the written details and enter the false owner's description.

The forgers who tamper with passports ought to give up now, however. Because a new kind of security paper has been developed on which anything that has been written can simply never be deleted. As the pen presses into the paper, besides releasing its own ink, it also releases secret ink. The security paper consists of four layers. The first of these is a conventional paper, next is a layer of tiny capsules of ink sealed in thin-

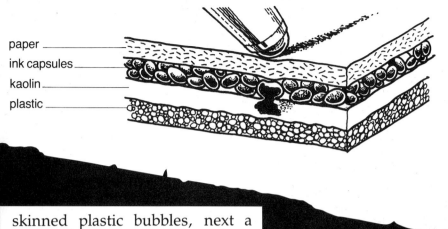

paper
ink capsules
kaolin
plastic

skinned plastic bubbles, next a layer of kaolin, a highly absorbent substance often used to soak up liquids, and finally a strong plastic base layer. When all four are tightly bonded together, you have what looks like a sheet of ordinary good quality paper. But pressure from a pen breaks the ink capsules, releasing ink into the kaolin layer which readily absorbs it. Because the bonding process actually draws the kaolin layer into the plastic, whatever is written is permanently embedded in every layer. Any attempt to remove it is doomed. Scratching or scraping to erase the writing simply breaks more ink capsules, and makes a complete mess of the paper. Removing any ink with bleach might lift off the ink of a normal pen from the top paper layer, but the kaolin and plastic layers cannot be reached by the bleach without the whole paper being destroyed.

In fact there is only one problem with the new paper: you dare not make a mistake when you write on it, because there is no possible way you can correct it!

Beating the Barnacles

I f you have ever found a penny washed up in the last dribbles
  of the waves that continually wash the shore at the seaside,
you will have noticed how bright and clean it is. This is because
copper very slowly dissolves in sea water. And you will have
observed a simple piece of chemistry that could perhaps help
prevent appalling accidents at sea.

For hundreds of years, huge iron and steel buoys have been
stationed in the sea to mark rocks or other hidden obstacles.

*Months of marine life fighting for
living space on the buoy can obscure
its vital message to sailors, but a
specially treated buoy can pass its
inspection with flying colours.*

Their painted colour codes tell ships' pilots whether to steer one side or the other. But in order to be effective, these buoys have to be visible from a long way off: and that means they need to be enormous, weighing several tonnes. After a while in the sea, all sorts of marine life – from barnacles to seaweed – tends to cling to the buoys, sometimes obscuring the navigational information. So these heavy iron and steel buoys have to be towed back to land at considerable expense and painstakingly cleaned up.

This is where the penny on the beach comes in. Copper in seawater produces a number of copper compounds poisonous to living things such as seaweed and barnacles. Why not, someone thought, coat the buoys in copper, so that it would dissolve in the sea slowly, keeping away barnacles and seaweed? It all sounded neat enough. But several problems made it look as though it was one of those bright ideas doomed to fail. First of all, even a thin coat of copper covering the lower half of the buoy would be more expensive than several cleaning trips. And second, a fundamental problem arose. When copper is directly attached to iron or steel, the electrolytic process which lets the copper dissolve in seawater no longer works.

But the idea was too good to give up entirely: and if a way could be found to use less copper and not rivet it to the buoy, and if it could be done cheaply, that would be a breakthrough. The first point realised is that less copper is used in a square metre of copper wire mesh than the same area of sheet copper. So that would be a way to save on copper. But how could it be fastened to the buoys? The next brainwave was to coat a wire copper mesh in plastic, then cut away the plastic on one side only, to expose the copper to the sea. The plastic on the other side would separate the copper from the iron of the buoy. Putting the mesh on to the buoy is as simple as putting on a string vest.

The best news of all is that it works. A test buoy suitably enmeshed in plastic-covered copper has been slowly leaking copper into the sea around it for over three years now – and there's not a barnacle in sight.

Seeing with Sound

Have you ever noticed how the sound of your voice varies in different places? Try singing your favourite song in the bathroom, recording it on a tape recorder about five metres away from you; and then do the same thing in the garden. The bathroom sound should be the fuller one – your garden voice will probably sound as though something is missing by comparison. And that is almost what has happened. In the open air, sound just travels away from you in all directions; but in a room it reaches the walls and bounces back. Because it cannot "escape" into thin air, the tape recorder will pick up more of your voice as it bounces back and forth around the room. That is because sound passes through the air as vibrations or sound waves, which gradually diminish as they travel further from the source and are reflected back, at least to some extent, by anything in their path.

The fact that sounds can bounce back off objects is of more than passing interest to the scientist. Because they can calculate, from the kind of differences you heard in your two songs, just how much sound has been absorbed by any surface it meets before being bounced back. And they can also calculate the variable distances that sound waves travel as they are reflected back from different parts of an uneven surface. For instance, if scientists put a coin on a postcard, identical sound waves directed at both the coin and postcard will be reflected back differently. The soft card will absorb more than the hard metal of the coin; and the few millimetres by which the top surface of the coin is higher than the surface of the card will also shorten the distance the sound has to travel. If the coin and the card are carefully scanned with the same sound wave, one point at a time, and the differences are measured as it is reflected back, then a picture of the coin and the card can be built up in terms of sound variations. Those sound variations can be translated into electrical signals to show a picture of the coin and the card on a television screen. This makes it possible to see, instead of hear, with the aid of sound.

The elaborate machinery of a microscope that uses sound. The wire carries an electrical signal which is converted into a sound wave, then focused by a special lens. Behind the wire is the mechanism for scanning this focused sound wave across the specimen being examined.

When your eyes can do the job directly, there is no obvious reason for creating pictures in this elaborate way. But often you cannot see into places which sound can reach. At high enough frequencies, although you cannot hear them, some sound waves can pass perfectly harmlessly through your flesh. It is these ultra-high frequencies, known as ultrasound, which are used to observe the way a baby is growing inside its mother's womb. The soundwaves pass through her abdomen and are reflected back from the baby. They build up a picture on a television screen, giving details for the doctor to study which could not have been seen so safely with X-rays. And in a similar way, doctors can see inside the body to look for diseases such as cancer. Ultrasound scanning has become a very important medical tool in the last few years.

But there is now an even more fascinating way in which "seeing with sound" has proved useful. Scientists are finding that it allows them to build microscopes with tremendous advantages over conventional optical microscopes, using lenses to magnify an object. To start with, conventional optical microscopes cannot distinguish depth. At the highest magnification, for instance, the face on a coin, stands out too much from the background for both to be in focus at once, and the eye cannot gauge the difference in depth between the two surfaces. An acoustic microscope, one using exceptionally high ultrasonic frequencies can show this very clearly. And it can also show living tissue as it really is. The optical microscope can only see tissue if it is prepared on a slide and then stained to show up features – so the tissue is dead and is not seen as it really is.

To make these acoustic microscopes work, however, takes some incredibly sophisticated technology. In order to examine the tiniest of objects, very high frequency sound waves have to be produced by passing electricity through what is called a piezo electric crystal. The sound waves it creates are scattered far too widely to focus on a tiny specimen under inspection. So the sound waves need to be focused, just as light waves are

The magic of the listening microscope: the twists and whirls reveal ridges and valleys on the uneven surface of a piece of paper when magnified, which a conventional microscope could not detect.

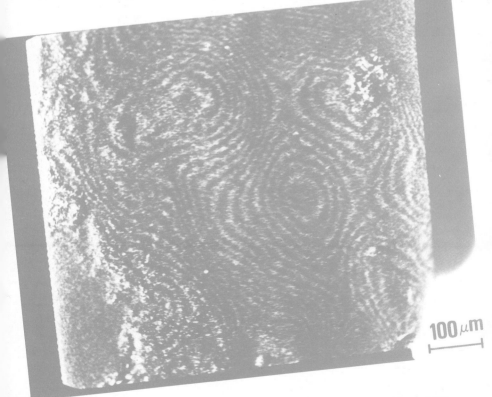

100 μm

focused through a lens. Water was tried, but it absorbs some of the sound as it passes through: and at very *very* high sound frequencies, virtually no sound gets through at all. This produces a poorer image than a high quality optical microscope. Therefore something less absorbent than water is needed, to focus the high frequency sounds. After trying liquid helium, an improvement on water, scientists are now convinced that other gases, contained under very high pressure, work even better.

The medical profession is eager to examine many kinds of living tissue under these sophisticated acoustic microscopes. It is easy to forget that a complex invention as this can be traced back to something as simple as singing in the bath.

Everlasting Plants

Three thousand years ago, in Ancient Egypt, some early scientists brewed up a potion with strange and wonderful properties. Applied to human flesh – which like all living matter soon rots away when a person has died – it will miraculously preserve a body virtually for ever. Embalmed with the magic solution, famous Egyptians have had their looks preserved for all of us to see thousands of years after they died.

Today, scientists in Sweden have taken over where the Egyptians left off. They have produced a new set of chemicals – still a trade secret – which include substances regularly used in the tinned meat industry, all mixed up with glycerine and water. And the con-

coction is then used to water plants. But not in any ordinary way. The roots of the plant are chopped off, the magic liquid is drawn up into the plant, and within seven days, the plant has been totally embalmed from the inside. The result – a permanent display of plants for the home or the office that need no watering, whose leaves do not fall off – and much more attractive than plastic flowers. But perhaps not as nice as live plants?

❀ ❀ ❀

Journey into Space

If there is one single advance in science and technology which has captured the minds of the world more than anything else, it is the exploration of space. Having been confined to the earth for millions of years, it is only in the last twenty or so that man has been able to travel beyond this planet. Men have stood on

the moon: machines have probed deeper into space and landed on or observed other planets at close quarters. And with all this spectacular science fact, there has blossomed, inevitably, a whole harvest of new science fiction. Films like "Star Wars" and "E.T. – The Extra Terrestrial" have shown us colonies in space at war with each other, or visitors from the planets of yet undiscovered galaxies. And we are captivated by them.

It makes it very difficult to look ahead realistically and assess just what tomorrow's world in space will be like. Technically,

there is almost no limit to what it is possible for men and women
to do: but politically and financially, there are very strong limits
on us. Even a single journey into space is colossally expensive.
It takes so much power to fire anything beyond the gravitation-
al pull of the earth that very few people can afford to finance
journeys into space. So far, the two most powerful countries in
the world, America and Russia, have done all the major
pioneering work, through government supported projects.
And all over the world people are questioning the value of

pouring more and more public funds into the space programmes when there are so many everyday problems to be solved on
earth. Reuseable spacecraft like the Shuttle have helped cut the
cost of each space flight: before this, all that returned to earth
was a tiny capsule from the nose of a giant rocket, containing
the astronauts. The vast engines and fuel systems which laun-
ched the rockets were abandoned in space or burned up in the
earth's atmosphere. But even the Shuttle has to lose one vast
fuel container as it breaks through the earth's atmosphere, and
will never be cheap to launch. So what is there to gain by
launching men into space?

To begin with, men on board the Shuttle can put satellites
into orbit around the earth, and adjust or maintain satellites
already there. Satellites are already used for a variety of pur-
poses, because they can look down on huge areas of the earth's
surface. With powerful cameras on board, they can send pictures back to earth to show how the weather is changing, or
what is happening at any hard-to-observe part of the world.
This means satellites are used for weather forecasting and
spying, as well as for building communications networks.
Radio, television and telephone signals between places as far
apart as London and Sydney, Tokyo and New York are relatively simply transmitted by sending them into space to a satellite,
where they are retransmitted back to the other side of the earth.
The alternative is a whole complex network of wires and cables
taking the signals around the curved surface of the earth. But
looking after satellites can only be a limited part of the space
programme. Once in place and working, satellites can last in
working order for several years, and do not require constant
visits from space crews.

Other ideas for making sense of the space programmes centre
around taking advantage of weightlessness, or the lack of
gravity, in space. Certain kinds of chemicals can only be made
by mixing ingredients together in such a way that the heavier
parts of the mixture do not sink to the bottom before the mixture
has had time to cool down or go through a series of chemical
changes. It would be ideal to mix these chemicals in space. But
is the colossal expense of getting them there worth it? At the
moment, various experiments on these lines are being tried on
flights of the Space Shuttle: but already many scientists are
saying that cheaper and equally effective ideas are being developed here on earth.

This leaves the one aspect of space travel that is perhaps the
most exciting of all to the imagination – exploration. Amazing

ideas that are technically possible have already suggested the possibility of men reaching out into corners of the universe we have not even seen yet. By taking men, machinery and raw materials back and forth into space, the argument goes, on regular Space Shuttle flights, we could build quite substantial bases in space. The Americans have quite realistic plans for a small experimental laboratory which would orbit the earth like a satellite, where scientists could spend a period of time at work before being taken back to the earth's surface. And beyond that, why not a bigger base – where a huge long-range spacecraft could be built? This would be big enough to take men and supplies further out into space where they could build the next space base – perhaps on the surface of another planet, or simply orbiting it just like the space base orbiting the earth. Gradually a whole chain of space bases could be built up, with men and supplies flown to and fro, until there were men and women living and breeding so far out in space that they could never return to the earth in their own lifetime. Ideas have been drawn up in some detail to show how huge spinning colonies in space

could be built where the spin created an artificial gravity for the colonists to walk normally; where a specially created artificial atmosphere would allow them to grow plants and survive indefinitely, rather like tropical fish in an aquarium.

The biggest drawback to the exciting possibilities of such an extraordinary new way of life is the vast expense of it. Since only the Americans and the Russians can afford today's limited space programmes and are already complaining of their cost, it is difficult to imagine the kind of changes that could happen to make the human race spend several million times more money on building space colonies.

But there again, it is unlikely that cavemen only a few thousand years ago believed that one day men would want to travel more than a few miles from the safety of their caves. And if you told them that men would walk on the moon, they could have laughed themselves silly. So who knows where our sense of adventure will take us?

Sugar for Cars

People may disagree about how quickly the world's oil resources will run out: but virtually everyone accepts that we have to find other sources of energy than petrol for our vehicles sooner or later. So all kinds of new fuels are being tried, either to replace or add to petrol. One unlikely source of experts for making new motor fuel was in a brewery. People who can convert hops and sugar with yeast, into beer, obviously know how to produce alcohol: and alcohol, if sufficiently pure, ought to burn in an unmodified car engine when mixed with petrol.

Brewers have used their experience to select the yeasts which will yield the maximum amount of alcohol as they ferment sugar. Wines and beers are made largely by fermenting the sugars produced naturally in the plant with yeasts that grow on the same plant: but since we want to brew fuel, not a drink, the careful nurturing of the right natural yeasts and sugar is not needed. (No one is bothered about the taste of fuel!) So a high yielding sugar plant – like sugar cane or sugar beet – is chopped up and mixed with the most vigorous yeasts. The chemistry of the process – bacteria in the yeasts digest the sugar to create

I'M NOT SURPRISED IT'S JERKING.....
YOU'RE RUNNING IT ON LUMP SUGAR!

alcohol and gas – leaves a liquid of which only 10% is alcohol. So the mixture is distilled. Effectively this means that a careful heating process evaporates the alcohol, which then separates from the rest of the liquid, and is collected and cooled down to become pure liquid alcohol. And this 100% alcohol has been added to petrol and used to help drive cars here in Britain very successfully. But it is not in the UK that growing sugar for fuel is going to prove an immediate success. The whole process is too expensive to compete with petrol prices at the moment. In other countries, however, where sugar grows in abundance quite easily, and they have no readily available supplies of crude oil, the attraction of brewing fuel for cars from their sugar is already being taken much more seriously. In South America, car engines have already been modified to run on pure alcohol derived from plant sugars. The day could come when brewers' skills will be appreciated for giving us more than fine wines and beers.

Gentle Switches

T he Queen and politicians would soon tire of their endless round of handshaking if every time they met someone new, they came to expect a sudden and painful powerful grip crunching their knuckles together. A firm but gentle handshake would be a rare pleasure. Surprisingly enough, although they cannot shake hands, light bulbs have to endure exactly that kind of treatment. Every time a light is switched on, it is more than likely that the filament wire in the bulb will be hit by a massive electrical current. A tiny current that gently builds up and makes the wire glow is as rare as the pleasurable handshake.

It all has to do with the nature of our electrical supply. In effect, over a very short period of time, it surges from zero volts to three hundred and forty, then drops down to zero again, then builds up to three hundred and forty volts again, then drops – and so on. Those voltage surges occur because domestic mains electricity flows one hundred times a second in opposite directions. That is why the current is called alternating current.

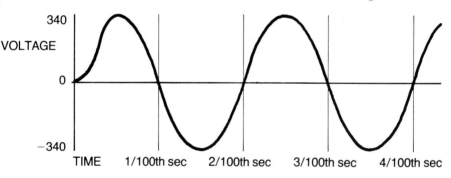

One hundred times every second the current is at zero volts then it changes direction, builds up and falls again. If only our light bulbs could be switched on at precisely the times when the current is at zero volts, then it would prevent the sudden shock of high voltages assaulting the thin wire filaments in the bulbs – which is what eventually wears them out. Obviously we cannot ourselves physically time our switching lights on to a critical fraction of a second, so a new kind of gentle switch has been invented. It depends on something called a triac and a computer. First, a computer analyses the mains current, and only allows the triac to be switched on at the precise moment when the current is approaching zero volts. The triac then connects up the lighting circuit, and the mains current always hits the bulb filament at a very low voltage.

Six or seven new ideas a week win the attention of the *Tomorrow's World* audience; over the last few pages you have been able to rediscover just a few of the more recent ones. Some are simple and ingenious; some weird, wonderful and worth at least a smile; others are complex, important and will change the world. In one way or another, this intriguing mixture of inventions and ingenuity gives a glimpse of the kind of world we can expect to live in tomorrow. But there is at least one key ingredient missing – ourselves. Because our decisions will determine which of these ideas live, and which perish. Will we accept or reject full scale nuclear power? Genetic engineering for perfect people? The technology already exists to do amazing things – but can we afford it? It is possible to imagine a world network of supersonic trains hurtling along at thousands of miles an hour, driven by magnetic forces in airless tubes to eliminate wind resistance. They could make aeroplanes obsolete – slow relics of a brief era of air travel. But it will cost a colossal amount to build such a rail network – and it will need the co-operation of all the governments of the world if the miles and miles of underground tunnels to house the vacuum train routes are ever to be built. Will we all agree to spend the money and forsake our political differences – or will we leave the vacuum bullet train as just another fantastic idea which never got off the drawing board?

The future could look enormously different – depending on the decisions we make. Will it be a world where everyone stays at home, unable to afford expensive fuel to travel anywhere, doing everything through a computerised telephone and video screen? Everyone could work from home, join school classes from home, even shop from home – by controlling remote video cameras to show you the produce you want to choose. Will it be a world where crippling diseases like cystic fibrosis and difficult inherited problems like haemophilia disappear with the help of genetic engineering? Or will we decide that altering our genes could also lead to less morally acceptable ends – such as breeding world champion football teams or super-brains? Science and technology will continue to supply us with countless possibilities to change our lives: as fast as the ideas arise, we will need to decide how to harness them. Tomorrow's World will be difficult, challenging – and inevitably exciting.

Alexandra Nowak

Völker zwischen Germanen und Kelten und die Festlegung der Rheingrenze

Kritik an schriftlichen und archäologischen Quellen

GRIN Verlag

Bibliografische Information der Deutschen Nationalbibliothek:

Die Deutsche Bibliothek verzeichnet diese Publikation in der Deutschen National-
bibliografie; detaillierte bibliografische Daten sind im Internet über http://dnb.d-
nb.de/ abrufbar.

Impressum:

Copyright © 2010 GRIN Verlag GmbH
Druck und Bindung: Books on Demand GmbH, Norderstedt Germany
ISBN: 978-3-656-02897-0

Dieses Buch bei GRIN:

http://www.grin.com/de/e-book/180150/voelker-zwischen-germanen-und-kelten-
und-die-festlegung-der-rheingrenze

Martin-Luther-Universität Halle-Wittenberg

Institut für Kunstgeschichte und Archäologien Europas

Methodisches Hauptseminar: Ausgewählte Probleme zur Frühgeschichte

Sommersemester 2008

Kritik an schriftlichen und archäologischen Quellen

- Völker zwischen Germanen und Kelten und die Festlegung der Rheingrenze -

von:

Alexandra von Rechenberg

8. Semester Geschichte/ 7. Semester Prähistorische Archäologie

1

Inhalt

1. Einleitung

„Germanien insgesamt ist von den Galliern, von den Rätern und Pannoniern durch Rhein und Donau, von den Sarmaten und Dakern durch wechselseitiges Mißtrauen oder Gebirgszüge geschieden".[1] So beschreibt Tacitus die Grenzen des *freien Germanien*.[2] Der Rhein trennt *Germanen* und *Kelten*. Was aber sind *Germanen* und *Kelten*? Sind sie archäologisch nachweisbar? Inwieweit fand diese Thematik Beachtung in der Forschung?

In der vorliegenden Arbeit sollen Antworten auf diese Fragen gefunden werden. Nach einem Überblick zur Forschungsgeschichte folgen die Zusammenstellung und Auswertung der Quellen. Begonnen wird mit den Schriftquellen. Es wird geklärt, welche schriftlichen Überlieferungen erhalten geblieben sind, was im Umgang mit ihnen zu beachten ist und welche Informationen sie zum Thema, Völker zwischen Germanen und Kelten und die Festlegung der Rheingrenze, liefern können. In Verbindung mit den Schriftquellen soll die Begriffsproblematik erläutert werden. Was bedeutet *Germane, Gallier* oder *Kelte*? Wer hat diese Begriffe geprägt und in welchem Kontext sind sie entstanden? Umfassen sie stets das gleiche oder wandelt sich ihre inhaltliche Bedeutung?

Nachfolgend sollen die archäologischen Funde und Befunde in den Gebieten westlich und östlich des mittleren und unteren Rhein vorgestellt und ausgewertet werden. Es wird untersucht, ob die Aussagen beider Quellengattungen synthetisierbar sind oder ob sie ein völlig konträres Bild ergeben. Weiterhin soll das Problem der ethnischen Interpretation beleuchtet werden. Lassen sich archäologische Sachgüter einer sozial und kulturell einheitlichen Gruppe zuordnen? Oder anders formuliert: Was sind Ethnien?

Zur Thematik *Germanen und Kelten* gibt es unüberschaubare Mengen an Literatur und ebenso viele unterschiedliche Ansätze im Umgang mit den Quellen und deren Interpretation.

Ein Beispiel ist das Werk von R. HACHMANN, G. KOSSACK und H. KUHN, *Völker zwischen Germanen und Kelten*, das 1962 erschienen ist. Es war für seine und die

---

[1] M. FUHRMANN, P. Cornelius Tacitus – Germania (Stuttgart 2000), Kap. 1. (Im Folgenden abgekürzt: Germ. Kap. 1).
[2] Damit werden die Gebiete jenseits von Rhein und Donau bezeichnet, die nicht römische Provinz waren.

nachfolgende Zeit innovativ. Beide Autoren[3] fassten zunächst alle Informationen aus den schriftlichen Überlieferungen zusammen und betrachteten anschließend das archäologische Fundgut. Für die Nachkriegszeit innovativ an dieser Vorgehensweise war, dass sie dabei die schriftlichen Quellen nicht als Grundlage nutzten, sondern archäologische und schriftliche Quellen gleichwertig nebeneinander stellten. Die Aussagen, die aufgrund beider Quellengattungen getroffen werden konnten, versuchten HACHMANN und KOSSACK abschließend zu vergleichen und zu verknüpfen. Bis 1945 und auch in den folgenden Jahrzehnten waren schriftliche Überlieferungen die Basis für die Erforschung der Besiedlung Mitteleuropas um Christi Geburt gewesen. Es wurden also zuerst diese Quellen ausgewertet und anschließend untersucht, ob die archäologischen Funde dazu passten bzw. wurden sie für passend gehalten.[4]

Aus diesem Grund sollen die Ansätze und Konzepte von HACHMANN und KOSSACK, sowie die kritische Auseinandersetzung damit neben dem Überblick zu den Quellen den Schwerpunkt dieser Arbeit bilden. Die Leitfragen sind:

1. War der Rhein kulturelle Grenze im ersten Jahrhundert v. Chr. bis in das erste Jahrhundert n. Chr.?

2. Existierten zu dieser Zeit am Rhein zwei Großgruppen - Germanen und Kelten - oder sind anhand der Quellen Belege für weitere verschiedene kulturelle Gruppen zu finden?

Das Thema „Völker zwischen Germanen und Kelten und die Festlegung der Rheingrenze" eignet sich gut, um die Grenzen der Aussagemöglichkeiten schriftlicher und archäologischer Quellen zu verdeutlichen. Zum einen sind für dieses Thema beide Quellengattungen vorhanden und zum anderen können grundlegende Forschungsprobleme, wie die Synthetisierbarkeit der Quellengattungen und die Problematik der ethnischen Deutung, vorgestellt werden. Die räumliche Rahmen ist durch den Titel der Arbeit benannt und die zeitliche Beschränkung auf das erste Jahrhundert v. Chr. bis zum ersten Jahrhundert n. Chr. gründet auf die historischen Ereignisse zu dieser Zeit. Im ersten Jahrhundert v. Chr. gelangte zum ersten Mal ein Römer bis an den Rhein. 58-49 v. Chr. unterwarf Gaius Iulius Caesar Gallien, wobei er auch in Kontakt zu Germanen trat und den Rhein als Ostgrenze

---

[3] Die Ausführungen KUHNS finden keine Beachtung, da in der vorliegenden Arbeit ausschließlich schriftliche und archäologische, jedoch keine philologischen Quellen, ausgewertet werden.
[4] Siehe Kapitel 2: *Forschungsgeschichtlicher Überblick.*

festlegte.[5]. Im Zuge des dessen wurde eine der wichtigsten schriftlichen Quellen zu Germanen und Kelten verfasst: *Commentarii de bello Gallico* von G. I. CAESAR. Durch die Unternehmungen von Augustus und Tiberius im ersten Jahrhundert n. Chr. östlich des Rheins blieb Germanien im Bewusstsein des römischen Volkes. So verfasste im ausgehenden ersten Jahrhundert n. Chr. P. C. TACITUS sein Werk: *De origine et situ Germanorum liber*, eine Beschreibung von Grenzen, Lebensgewohnheiten und anderer Charakteristika der Germanen.

Die beiden wichtigsten schriftlichen Quellen für die vorliegende Arbeit stammen aus dem ersten Jahrhundert v. Chr. und dem ersten Jahrhundert n. Chr., womit die Festlegung des zeitlichen Rahmens erklärt ist.

---

[5]Vgl. hierzu die Kurzübersicht der Ereignisse bei W. SCHLÜTER, Kalkriese - Ort der Varusschlacht? Die Ausgrabungen in der Kalkrieser-Niewedder Senke. In: M. FANSA (Hrsg.), Varusschlacht und Germanenmythos. Eine Vortragsreihe anläßlich der Sonderausstellung Kalkriese – Römer im Osnabrücker Land 1993 (Oldenburg 1994) 11 f.

2. Forschungsgeschichtlicher Überblick

Die sich entwickelnde Archäologie des 19. Jahrhunderts vertraute ohne Einwände den antiken schriftlichen Quellen. Bereits in den 80er Jahren des 19. Jahrhunderts beschäftigte sich G. KOSSINNA mit der vorgeschichtlichen Ausbreitung der Germanen.[6] Er suchte in den historischen Quellen nach Hinweisen für deren Siedlungsgebiete im Raum (der heutigen Bundesrepublik) Deutschlands. Alle archäologischen Funde in diesen Gebieten waren für ihn germanisch. Frühe Formen entsprachen ersten Siedlungsgebieten.[7] K. SCHUMACHER wandte KOSSINNAS Vorgehensweise für Kelten an.[8]

Kritik an KOSSINNA und SCHUMACHER übten K. SCHULLER und E. WAHLE.[9] Sie waren der Ansicht, dass ein Bevölkerungswechsel eintreten könne, ohne dass dies an Bodenfunden sichtbar werde. Ebenso kritisierten sie, dass sich SCHUMACHER und KOSSINNA nur mit je einer Quellengattung beschäftigten, ohne die Übereinstimmungen und Widersprüchlichkeiten im Aussagegehalt der verschiedenen Quellengattungen zu berücksichtigen und zu interpretieren.[10]

Die Diskussion über die Siedlungsgebiete der Germanen begann zuerst in der skandinavischen Archäologie mit O. MONTELIUS u. a.[11] Er beschäftigte sich mit der Einwanderung germanischer Gruppen/Stämme o. ä. (Vorfahren) in Schweden und Norwegen und vermutete ihren Ursprung in den Gebieten um das Schwarze Meer und an der unteren Donau.[12] Etwa zeitgleich befasste sich KOSSINNA seit seiner Dissertation 1881 mit der germanischen Besiedlungsgeschichte, da aber noch ausschließlich philologisch.[13] In den 20er Jahren des 20. Jahrhunderts entwickelte er seinen methodischen Hauptsatz: „Scharf umgrenzte archäologische Kulturprovinzen

---

[6] R. HACHMANN, Germanen und Kelten am Rhein in der Zeit um Christi Geburt. In: R. HACHMANN, G. KOSSACK, H. KUHN, Völker zwischen Germanen und Kelten (Neumünster 1962), 12.
[7] Ebd.
[8] K. SCHUMACHER, Siedlungs- und Kulturgeschichte der Rheinlande von der Urzeit bis in das Mittelalter (Mainz 1921).
[9] HACHMANN, 1962, 12. Vgl. auch: E. WAHLE, Zur ethnischen Deutung frühgeschichtlicher Kulturprovinzen (Heidleberg 1941); E. WAHLE, Grenzen der frühgeschichtlichen Erkenntnis (Heidelberg 1941); E. WAHLE, Deutsche Vorzeit (Basel 1952).
[10] Ebd.
[11] H. JANKUHN, Das Germanenproblem in der älteren archäologischen Forschung. In: H. BECK (Hrsg.), Germanenprobleme in heutiger Sicht (Berlin/ New York 1986), 298.
[12] JANKUHN, 1986, 298 ff.
[13] G. KOSSINNA, Über die ältesten hochfränkischen Sprachdenkmäler – Ein Beitrag zur Grammatik des Althochdeutschen (veröffentlichte Dissertation), (Straßburg 1881).

6

decken sich zu allen Zeiten mit ganz bestimmten Völkern und Völkerstämmen."[14]

Nach KOSSINNA sei die Urheimat der Germanen an der mittleren Donau zu suchen. Von dort hätten sie sich Oder- und Elbe abwärts ausgebreitet. Spätestens zu Beginn des 3. Jahrtausends v. Chr. siedelten Germanen, so KOSSINNA, in Mecklenburg, Schleswig-Holstein, Dänemark und Südschweden. KOSSINNA wie MONTELIUS gingen von einer ungebrochenen Kontinuität germanischer Besiedlung vom Neolithikum bis zur Bronzezeit aus.[15]

Obwohl es bereits seit den 20er Jahren des 20. Jahrhunderts neue Ansätze zur Siedlungsarchäologischen Methode KOSSINNAS gab, bei denen mehr Wert auf die Untersuchung der Siedlung selbst/die archäologischen Funde und Befunde gelegt wurde[16], war vor allem im Dritten Reich KOSSINNAS Methode maßgebend.[17]

Sämtliche Interpretationsansätze der Germanen- und Keltenforschung gingen von einheitlichen Kulturgruppen aus, die den historisch überlieferten Völkern entsprechen.

Auch R. VON USLAR gibt an, schriftliche Quellen stellten die Grundlage dar auf der die weitere Forschung aufbauen müsse.[18] Für ihn ist es problematisch, Bodenfunde eines abgegrenzten Raumes von vornherein einem Stammesgebiet zuzuordnen.[19]

Hauptprobleme der Germanenforschung im 20. Jahrhundert, auch in den Nachkriegsjahrzehnten, sind unter anderem die ethnische Deutung, d. h. die Gleichsetzung archäologisch fassbarer Kulturen mit historisch überlieferten politischen Verbänden und Stammesgruppen und die Definition des Wortes *Germane*.[20] WAHLE beispielsweise betonte, dass Fundprovinzen sich mit Ethnien decken können, aber nicht müssen.[21] Vertreten wurde weitgehend die Theorie, ein archäologisch einheitlicher Kulturraum kann mit aus der Antike überlieferten Stämmen gleichgesetzt werden (Abb. 1).[22] Aber die Diskussion um die ethnische

---

[14] G. KOSSINNA, Die Herkunft der Germanen. Zur Methode der Siedlungsarchäologie (Leipzig 1920), 3.
[15] JANKUHN, 1986, 304.
[16] Hier zu nennen sei H. JANKUHN, Einführung in die Siedlungsarchäologie (Berlin/ New York 1977).
[17] Da KOSSINNAS Vorstellungen von einem überlegenen germanischen Volk in Einklang mit der nationalsozialistischen Ideologie war, konnten sich andere (schlüssige) Ansätze nicht durchsetzen.
[18] R. VON USLAR, Westgermanische Bodenfunde. In: Römisch Germanische Kommission (Hrsg.), Germanische Denkmäler der Frühzeit (Berlin 1938), 173.
[19] VON USLAR, 1938, 174.
[20] G. MILDENBERGER, Die Germanen in der archäologischen Forschung nach KOSSINNA. In: H. BECK (Hrsg.), Germanenprobleme in heutiger Sicht (Berlin/ New York 1986), 310.
[21] WAHLE, 1941a, 14.
[22] MILDENBERGER, 1986, 311.

Deutung ist problematisch, da nach wie vor nicht geklärt ist, was unter *germanisch* zu verstehen ist.

Das Thema der vorliegenden Arbeit ist in der Forschung hauptsächlich aus der „germanischen Richtung" zu erschließen. Alle Werke, die sich mit Germanen und Kelten am Rhein im ersten Jahrhundert v. Chr. und im ersten Jahrhundert n. Chr. befassen, setzen den Schwerpunkt auf die germanische Besiedlung dieser Gebiete.

3. Völker zwischen Germanen und Kelten am Rhein - Quellenlage

3. 1. Schriftquellen

Im folgenden Kapitel werden die beiden wichtigsten schriftlichen Quellen über die germanische Besiedlung westlich und östlich des mittleren und unteren Rhein im ersten Jahrhundert v. Chr. bis zum ersten Jahrhundert n. Chr. vorgestellt: *Commentarii de bello Gallico* von G. I. CAESAR und *De origine et situ Germanorum* (kurz: *Germania*) von P. C. TACITUS. Die Werke dieser beiden Autoren beinhalten die prägnantesten Informationen, sodass weiniger ergiebige Quellen im Rahmen dieser Untersuchung keine Berücksichtigung finden. Diese Quellen sind ausreichend, um zu erläutern, wie schriftliche Quellen ausgewertet werden.

3. 1. 1. G. I. CAESAR – COMMENTARII DE BELLO GALLICO

Unter Beachtung folgender Fragen soll CAESARS Werk ausgewertet werden: Was wird mitgeteilt zum Rhein als Grenze? Ist eine klare Trennung zwischen keltischen und germanischen Siedlungsgebieten erkennbar anhand der Quelle? Gibt es weitere kulturelle Gruppen außer *Germanen* und *Kelten*?

Commentarii de bello Gallico ist ein Bericht über den Gallischen Krieg (58 – 51/ 50 v. Chr.). Er besteht aus acht Büchern, wobei ein Buch einem Kriegsjahr entspricht. CAESAR beginnt mit einer ethnographischen und geographischen Beschreibung Galliens. Es folgt eine Schilderung des Gallischen Krieges, der mit dem Feldzug gegen die Helvetier beginnt.[23] Relevant ist Buch VI, 11-28. Es beinhaltet einen Vergleich zwischen Gallien und Germanien, insbesondere die Abschnitte 24-25. Einige wenige Informationen können aus Buch I, 31 und Buch IV, 1-4 gewonnen werden:

Aus Buch I, 31 ist zu erfahren, dass ungefähr 15 000 Germanen den Rhein überquert haben sollen, „Ackerbau, Zivilisation und Reichtum der Gallier [hätten] schätzen [ge]lern[t]", worauf hin mehr gekommen seien und nun 120 000 Germanen in Gallien lebten.

---

[23] M. DEISSMANN, De bello Gallico. Lateinisch-Deutsch (Stuttgart 1995), 90. Die Quelle wird im Folgenden mit „B. G. Buch, Abschnitt" abgekürzt.

Im vierten Kriegsjahr „überschritten die germanischen Stämme der Usipeter und Tenkterer in großer Zahl den Rhein nahe dem Ort, wo er in die Nordsee mündet", so CAESAR weiter.[24] Die Ubier seien „für germanische Verhältnisse ein großes und blühendes Volk (...). Sie [seien] etwas zivilisierter als die übrigen Germanen, weil ihr Gebiet an den Rhein stößt (...). Wegen der Nähe zu Gallien [hätten] sie selbst gallische Sitten angenommen.".[25] Usipeter und Tencterer seien von Sueben vertrieben worden und gelangten an den Rhein.[26] Dort würden auch Menapier wohnen, die zu beiden Seiten des Rheins Siedlungen besäßen.[27] Die Ankunft der Usipeter und Tencterer hätte die Menapier zur Flucht veranlasst. Sie hätten „ihre Gehöfte jenseits des Flusses" verlassen.[28] Usipetern und Tencteren sei es jedoch gelungen den Rhein zu überqueren und die Menapier zu überwältigen.[29]

Aus dem Vergleich zwischen Gallien und Germanien ist zu entnehmen, dass Gallier einst jenseits des Rheins Kolonien gründeten.[30] Die fruchtbarsten Gebiete Germaniens lägen im Bereich des herkynischen Waldes.[31] „Die Ausdehnung des hercynischen Waldes, (...), [entspräche] einem zügigen Fußmarsch ohne Gepäck von neun Tagen (...).[32] „Der Wald beginnt im Gebiet der Helvetier, Nemeter und Rauracer und erstreckt sich in gerader Richtung auf die Donau zu bis zum Gebiet der Dacer und Anatier."[33] Es gäbe niemanden, „der von sich behaupten könnte, er sei bis zum östlichen oder nordöstlichen Rand des Waldes vorgestoßen, auch wenn er sechzig Tage marschiert wäre, noch weiß jemand, wo der Wald anfängt".[34]

---

[24] B. G. IV, 1.
[25] B. G. IV, 3.
[26] B. G. IV, 4.
[27] Ebd.
[28] Ebd. Jenseits bedeutet östlich.
[29] B. G. IV, 4.
[30] B. G. VI, 24.
[31] Ebd.
[32] B. G. VI, 25.
[33] Ebd.
[34] Ebd. Der herkynische Wald muss Caesars Schilderungen zufolge beträchtliche Ausmaße gehabt haben. Angenommen pro Tag seien 20 km zu bewältigen, so sind das bei einem Fußmarsch von neun Tagen 180 km. Der östlich und nordöstliche Rand jedoch wurde noch nicht erreicht, auch bei einem Marsch von 60 Tagen nicht (entspricht etwa einer Ausdehnung von 1200km. Es muss aber beachtet werden, dass geographische Angaben schwer nachvollziehbar sind, da die Vegetation vor 2000 Jahren wahrscheinlich eine andere war als gegenwärtig. Allein dadurch, dass um Christi Geburt vermutlich der größte Teil Mitteleuropas mit Wäldern bedeckt war, wäre es nicht verwunderlich, wenn der herkynische Wald eine derartige Größe besessen hätte.

10

Mehrfach wurde der Versuch unternommen, CAESARS Motivation für die Niedrschrift von *De bello Gallico* zu erschließen. Nachvollziehbar sind die Angaben von W. M. ZEITLER. Im Falle von CAESARS Sieg, sei sein Ruhm nach des Feindes Unterwerfung umso größer, je schlimmer der Feind.[35] Für den Fall der Niederlage führt Zeitler an, da die Germanen so unzivilisiert und wild seien, seien sie es auch nicht wert, dass ihr Land erobert werde.[36] Anzunehmen ist weiterhin, dass die *commentarii* zur Darstellung und Profilierung der Person CAESARS gedacht waren. Sein Bericht könnte als „Mittelweg zwischen geschichtlicher Schilderung und Propaganda in eigener Sache" bezeichnet werden.[37] Seine Aufzeichnungen sollten vor allem bezwecken, die Notwendigkeit seines Feldzuges dem römischen Senat gegenüber zu erklären und somit seinen Krieg zu rechtfertigen.[38] Sein Werk ist also von starken Eigeninteressen geprägt und keineswegs objektiv.

Gleichermaßen problematisch ist der Umstand, dass CAESAR lediglich zweimal den Rhein überschritt und dabei vermutlich nicht weit ins Landesinnere vordringen konnte. Er vertraute für die Gebiete östlich des Rheins sowohl keltischen Überlieferungen als auch Mitteilungen römischer Boten, Spähtrupps und Diplomaten. Dabei ist zu beachten, dass die keltischen Beschreibungen wahrscheinlich eine Abgrenzung gegenüber allem Germanischen betonen. Wird eine fremdartige Gruppe beschrieben, konzentrieren sich die Beschreibungen vor allem auf das Fremdartige, was dann als typisch gilt.[39] Das könnte dazu geführt haben, dass CAESARS Bild vom wilden, unberechenbaren Germanen noch bestätigt wurde. Für die Gebiete westlich des Rheins konnte er auch eigene Erfahrungen sammeln.[40]

Schwierig ist es, zu erfassen, was hinter CAESARS Germanenbegriff stand. Für HACHMANN beispielsweise war der Begriff keine Realität, sondern gelehrte Konstruktion.[41] Auch für H. AMENT: Gallien endete am Rhein. Alles jenseits davon war für CAESAR Germanien. Der Rhein war eher politische als ethnographische

---

[35] W. M. ZEITLER, Zum Germanenbegriff Caesars. In: H. BECK (Hrsg.), Germanenprobleme in heutiger Sicht (Berlin/ New York 1986), 43.
[36] ZEITLER, 1986, 43.
[37] DEISSMANN, 1995, 94.
[38] DEISSMANN, 1995, 94.
[39] A. A. LUND, Zum Germanenbegriff bei Tacitus. In: H. Beck (Hrsg.), Germanenprobleme in heutiger Sicht (Berlin/ New York 1986), 54.
[40] K. PESCHEl, Kelten und Germanen während der jüngeren vorrömischen Eisenzeit (2. – 1. Jh. v. Chr.) (Berlin1988), 167.
[41] HACHMANN, 1962, 32.

Grenze[42], was m. E. zustimmt. Vermutlich war alles rechts des Rheins germanisch. Allerdings taucht in den *commentarii* die Bezeichnung *Germani cisrhenani* auf.[43] Da CAESAR sie gesamt als *Germani* bezeichnete, galten sie anscheinend als den rechtrheinischen Germanen verwandt.[44] Ob ursprünglich Kelten diese Bezeichnung prägten, ist unklar.[45] Letztendlich wird es nicht mehr nachvollziehbar sein, was CAESARS Begriff umfasste.[46]

Ab wann und ob überhaupt sich die Germanen selbst als Germanen bezeichnet haben ist nicht belegt, gleichwohl es in der Literatur andere Angaben gibt. So schreibt AMENT, dass der Begriff zunächst von Galliern geprägt worden sei und dann jedoch von Germanen übernommen wurde.[47]

Bei TACITUS[48] heißt es, dass der Begriff *Germane* neu sei: „Denn die ersten, die den Rhein überschritten und die Gallier vertrieben hätten, die jetzigen Tungrer, seien damals Germanen genannt wurden. So habe der Name eines Stammes, nicht eines ganzen Volkes, allmählich weite Geltung erlangt: zuerst wurden alle nach dem Sieger, aus Furcht vor ihm, als Germanen bezeichnet, bald aber nannten auch sie selbst sich so, nachdem der Name einmal aufgekommen war.[49]

3. 1. 2. P. C. TACITUS – ORIGINE ET SITU GERMANORUM LIBER

Die zweite der beiden wichtigsten Schriftquellen hinsichtlich der Frage nach den Siedlungsräumen der Germanen und deren Abgrenzung von anderen Gruppierungen ist die *Germania* des TACITUS. Darin beschreibt er das *freie Germanien*, also die Gebiete östlich des Rheins, die nicht römische Provinz waren. Sein Werk lässt sich in zwei Teile gliedern. Der erste berichtet von den Grenzen Germaniens[50], vom Ursprung der Germanen[51], vom germanischen Kriegswesen[52], von ihrem

---

[42] H. AMENT, Unterwegs zu höherer Zivilisation – Die Germanen. In: W. SCHULLER, Frühe Völker Europas (Stuttgart 2003), 44.
[43] G. NEUMANN, Germani cisrhenani – die Aussage der Namen. In: H. BECK (Hrsg.), Germanenprobleme in heutiger Sicht (Berlin/ New York 1986), 107.
[44] NEUMANN, 1986, 107.
[45] NEUMANN, 1986, 107.
[46] Die damit zusammenhängende Problematik der ethnischen Deutung wird im Kapitel 3. 2. *Archäologische Quellen* erläutert.
[47] AMENT, 2003, 45.
[48] Im Anschluss an *De bello Gallico* folgt die Auswertung der Taciteischen *Germania*.
[49] M. FUHRMANN, P. Cornelius Tacitus – Germania (Stuttagrt 2000), Kap. 2. Im Folgenden abgekürzt: Germ. Kap. 2.
[50] Germ. Kap. 1.
[51] Germ. Kap. 2.
[52] Germ. Kap. 6.

Siedlungswesen[53] u.a. Im zweiten Teil beschreibt TACITUS die einzelnen Stämme und ihre Besonderheiten.[54]

Die Grenzen Germaniens sollen die Donau im Süden und der Rhein im Westen, das Weltmeer mit Dänemark und Skandinavien im Norden und im Osten die Weichsel und Siebenbürgen bilden.[55] Im Westen (Germaniens) würden Gallier siedeln.[56] Zwischen dem herkynischem Wald[57], Rhein und Main sollen Helvetier und Bojer (gallische Stämme) leben.[58] Das Rheinufer selbst würden germanische Stämme bewohnen: Vangionen, Triboker und Nemeter.[59] Ubier hätten den Rhein überschritten und wären unmittelbar am Ufer des Rheins von Römern angesiedelt worden, da diese sich Rom gegenüber als treu erwiesen hätten.[60]

Ein weiterer germanischer Stamm, die Bataver, seien am tapfersten, so Tacitus. Sie sollen einen Streifen am linken Ufer des Rheins und die Rheininsel bewohnen.[61] Matthiaker würden jenseits des Rheins leben.[62]

Den herkynischen Wald beschrieb Tacitus als Wohnsitz der Chatten.[63] Neben diesen sollen am Rhein Usipeter und Tenkterer siedeln.[64] In der Nähe der Tenkterer hätten einst Brukterer gelebt. Sie wären allerdings von Chamavern und Angrivariern ausgerottet worden, die sich diese Gebiete einverleibt hätten.[65] Südöstlich von beiden eben genannten Stämmen hätten Dulgubnier und Chasuarier gesiedelt, „sowie andere, weniger bekannte Stämme".[66] Nördlich von diesen Stämmen hätten Friesen gelebt und in deren Nähe Chauken.[67] Nachbarn der Chauken und Chatten seien Cherusker gewesen, benachbarter Stamm derer wären die Foser gewesen.[68]

Damit wären alle Informationen zur Besiedlung der Rheinufer anhand der *Germania* zusammengetragen. Die nachfolgenden Ausführungen beziehen sich auf

---

[53] Germ. Kap. 16.
[54] Germ. Kap. 28.
[55] Germ. Kap. 1. Die Bezeichnungen „Siebenbürgen" etc. entsprechen den Angaben des Verfassers der zitierten Ausgabe der *Germania*: FUHRMANN, 2000, 71-92.
[56] Germ. Kap. 28.
[57] Nach FUHRMANN umfasst der herkynische Wald den Spessart, den Vogelsberg, die Rhön und die Weserberge. FUHRMANN, 2000, 85. Er ist bereits bei Caesar erwähnt (siehe Kapitel 3. 1. 1. *G. I. CAESAR – Commentarii de bello Gallico*).
[58] Germ. Kap. 28.
[59] Ebd.
[60] Germ. Kap. 28.
[61] Germ. Kap. 29. Welche Rheininsel Tacitus angesprochen hat, ist nicht klar.
[62] Germ. Kap. 29. Jenseits des Rheins bedeutet in antiken Schriften östlich des Rheins.
[63] Germ. Kap. 30.
[64] Germ. Kap. 32.
[65] Germ. Kap. 33.
[66] Germ. Kap. 34.
[67] Germ. Kap. 34/ 35.
[68] Germ. Kap. 36.

germanische Stämme weiter im Landesinneren, die nicht in der Nähe des Rheins ihre Siedlungsgebiete hatten und daher irrelevant für das Thema der Arbeit sind. Zusammenfassend ist festzuhalten, dass TACITUS über fast ausschließlich östlich des Rheins siedelnde germanische Stämme berichtet. Eine Ausnahme bildeten vermutlich die Ubier. Der Quelle zu entnehmen ist, dass sie den Rhein überschritten und dass sie von Römern am Ufer des Rheins angesiedelt wurden. Allerdings ist unklar, an welchem Ufer. Angenommen sie wurden am westlichen Rheinufer angesiedelt, während sie damit der einzige westlich des Rheins siedelnde germanische Stamm nach TACITUS.

TACITUS selbst war nie am Rhein oder in den Gebieten östlich des Flusses. Seine Kenntnisse erhielt er vermutlich von Landsleuten (Soldaten oder Handelsleuten) und aus vorhergegangenen Berichten (literarischen Werken) von J. Caesar (*De bello Gallico*) und wahrscheinlich jetzt verlorene Schriften des Livius' (*Geschichtswerk* Buch 104) und des älteren Plinius' (*Germanische Kriege*).[69]

Nach wie vor umstritten sind die Gründe für die Entstehung der *Germania*.. Sie sind umso schwieriger zu fassen, weil das Werk keine Einleitung hat, in der der Autor seine Motive eventuell mitgeteilt hätte. Schlüssig ist m. E. die moralische Begründung. TACITUS habe den Römern einen Spiegel vorhalten wollen, da ihre Dekadenz ihr Verderben ist.[70] Er sah das Ideal einer Gesellschaft in der Reinheit und Ursprünglichkeit des Zusammenlebens germanischer Stämme. Er lobt ihr ehrliches Wesen[71], ihre Größe und Kraft[72] und ihren Sinn für Ehre[73]. Aber allein eine Huldigung germanischer Eigenschaften ist die *Germania* nicht. Er rügt auch Trunksucht und Würfelspiel.[74]

Auch TACITUS' Germanenbegriff ist schwierig zu fassen. Zwar handelt es sich nicht wie bei Caesar, um einen rein politischen Begriff, der einen bestimmten Feind bezeichnete. Aber ob es sich um ein tatsächlich vorhandenes, kulturell einheitliches Gebilde handelte, ist fragwürdig.

Im Anschluss an die archäologischen Quellen soll auf die *ethnische Deutung* näher eingegangen werden.

---

[69] Fuhrmann, 2000, 100.
[70] Lund, 1986, 33.
[71] Germ. Kap. 22.
[72] Germ. Kap. 20.
[73] Germ. Kap. 14.
[74] Germ. Kap. 23/ 24.

3. 2. Archäologische Quellen

Der archäologische Befund am Rhein ist für das erste Jahrhundert v. Chr. und für das erste Jahrhundert n. Chr. Für das archäologische Fundgut gibt es in der Literatur keinen Überblick. Daher ist es nicht möglich zu erfahren, welche Funde explizit in diesem Gebiet entdeckt wurden. Zahlreiche unterschiedliche Interpretationen sorgen ebenfalls für einen schwierigen Zugang zum Thema. Einige davon sollen im Folgenden vorgestellt werden, denn nur über diese theoretischen Ansätze gelingt es, etwas zum archäologischen Material zu erfahren.

Für seine Zeit ungwöhnlich, ist WAHLE der Ansicht, dass Vermischungen von verschiedenen Kulturgütren/Kulturgütern verschiedner Provenienz möglich und eine scharfe Abgrenzung derselben voneinander nicht immer realisierbar sei.[75] Er weist darauf hin, dass ein archäologischer Fund ein zufällig erhaltener Rest der einstigen materiellen Kultur sei.[76] Er widerspricht damit den in den 30er und 40er Jahren des 20. Jahrhunderts den populären Ideen KOSSINNAS.[77] Zwar sind WAHLES Zweifel an der eindeutigen Zuordnung von archäologischen Funden für seine Schaffenszeit fortschrittlich, aber seine Äußerungen zu den Germanen allgemein sind diskutabel. So gibt er an, dass bereits 700 v. Chr. Germanen rechts des Niederrheins siedelten. Er begründet dies mit dem Vorkommen von Urnengräbern und spärlichen Bronzen.[78] Nach Stand der 60er Jahre des 20. Jahrhunderts kann von drei germanischen Siedlungsgruppen am Oberrhein gesprochen werden: 1. Groß – Gerauer Gruppe, 2. Diesheimer Gruppe, 3. Unteres Neckarland Gruppe.[79] Diese sind mutmaßlich zu den Elbgermanen zugehörig.[80] Die beiden Gruppen um Groß Gerau und im unteren Neckarland sind wohl um Christi Geburt in diese Gebiete gelangt.[81] Doch bereits in der Mitte des ersten Jahrhunderts n. Chr. gibt es kein germanisches Fundgut mehr am Oberrhein, was mit der dortigen römischen Machtausbreitung begründet wird.[82] Lediglich die Diersheimer Gruppe nimmt ab der zweiten Hälfte des 2. Jahrhunderts

---

[75] WAHLE, 1941a, 8.
[76] Dem widersprechen Grab- und Hortfunde. Diese nicht „zufällig".
[77] Vgl. Kapitel 2. *Forschungsgeschichtlicher Überblick.*
[78] WAHLE, 1941a, 29. Unklar ist, wie das Vorkommen von Urnengräbern und spärlichen Bronzen die Anwesenheit von Germanen belegen soll, zumal sich die Frage stellt, was „spärliche Bronzen" sind. Abbildungen dazu sind ebenfalls nicht vorhanden.
[79] R. NIERHAUS, Das suebische Gräberfeld von Diersheim. In: Römische – Germanische Forschungen, 28 (Berlin 1966), 183.
[80] NIERHAUS, 1966, 195.
[81] Ebd.
[82] Ebd.

15

wieder Kontakt zum elbgermanischen Bereich auf.[83] Dennoch ist bei der Fundzuweisung Vorsicht geboten, da eine Vermischung von keltischem und germanischem Kulturgut am Rhein wahrscheinlich und nicht immer klar zu trennen ist.[84]

In den 80er Jahren des letzten Jahrhunderts wird die Jastorfkultur als germanisch interpretiert.[85] Jedoch ist sich V. PETRIKOVITZ nicht sicher, ob sich dahinter ein ethnisch einheitlicher Träger verbirgt.[86] Nach K. PESCHEL ist dem archäologischen Kontext folgend eine ethnische Zweiteilung belegbar.[87] Nördlich der Alpen bis an den Main und Mittelböhmen siedelt die Oppidakultur der frühen Latènezeit; nördlich der Mittelgebirge, am Mittel- und Unterlauf der Elbe siedelten die Träger der Jastorfkultur, wobei die Jastorfkultur als Quelle dessen angesehen wird, was als germanisch gilt.[88] Für PESCHEL ist sicher, dass vieles vom Sachgut der vorrömischen Eisenzeit im Norden Deutschlands zwischen Niederrhein und Weichsel der elbgermanischen Kultur zugehörig ist.[89] Vereinfachend gesagt, war der Süden auf dem Gebiet des heutigen Deutschlands keltisch, der Nordosten elbgermanisch. Im Nordwesten zeigten sich anhand der Bodenfunde Besonderheiten: die Prägung der Rhein-Weser-germanischen Gruppe durch die materielle Kultur des kaiserzeitlichen Römischen Imperiums.[90] Zwar gibt PESCHEL selbst an, die Vorstellung von einer Einheit der Germanen entstamme wohl eher politischem Denken, jedoch seien im Elbgebiet Übereinstimmungen zwischen schriftlichen und archäologischen Quellen in den ersten zwei Jahrhunderten n. Chr. zu erkennen.[91] Damit ist nicht der Wohnbezirk eines einzelnen Stammes gemeint, vielmehr ein „Wirtschaftsraum" mit gleichartigen Zügen der materiellen und geistigen Kultur.[92] Es gibt aber keine scharfen Grenzen, eher regionale Besonderheiten: Für die Elbgermanen typisch sind, PESCHEL weiter folgend, Trichterurnen. Trotz gleicher Grundformen, zeigen sich

---

[83] NIERHAUS, 1966, 195. Generell problematisch ist das Fehlen von genauen Angaben zu den archäologischen Funden, die die jeweilige Theorie bekräftigen sollen. Somit sind sämtliche Aussagen von z. B. Nierhaus nicht nachzuvollziehen.

[84] NIERHAUS, 1966, 199-212.

[85] H. V. PETRIKOVITZ, Germani cisrhenani. In: H. BECK (Hrsg.), Germanenprobleme in heutiger Sicht (Berlin/ New York 1986), 98.

[86] V. PETRIKOVITZ, 1986, 98.

[87] K. PESCHEL, Kelten und Germanen während der jüngeren vorrömischen Eisenzeit (2.-1. Jahrhundert v. Chr.). In: F. HORST, F. SCHLETTE (Hrsg.), Frühe Völker in Mitteleuropa (Berlin 1988), 167.

[88] PESCHEL, 1988, 168. Es ist nicht nachzuvollziehen, wie PESCHEL zu der Annahme kommt, aus der Jastorfkultur haben sich Germanen entwickelt., da keine Funde angegeben werden.

[89] K. PESCHEL, Anfänge germanischer Besiedlung im Mittelgebirgsraum. In: Arbeits- und Forschungsberichte zur sächsischen Bodendenkmalpflege, 12 (Berlin 1978), 5.

[90] PESCHEL, 1988, 168.

[91] PESCHEL, 1978, 17-21.

[92] PESCHEL, 1978, 21.

16

Unterschiede insofern, dass an der Niederelbe eine breite Schulterwölbung der Gefäße fassbar sei, während bspw. in Thüringen die Gefäßschulter verkürzt und kantig ausgeprägt sei.[93]

Bei V. PETRIKOVITZ wird der Rhein als Grenze verstanden, da germanische Bevölkerungen bis in die Gebiete östlich des Rheins vorgedrungen seien, ohne diesen zu überschreiten.[94] Auch AMENT vertritt die Annahme, dass anhand archäologischer Funde der Rhein nicht als „Völkerscheide" gesehen werden kann.[95] Ansonsten lässt sich bei den anderen genannten Autoren nicht eindeutig erkennen, ob sie den Rhein als Grenze verstehen. Anerkannter Konsens ist jedoch, mit einer Ausnahme[96], ihr Konzept von der ethnischen Einheit der Germanen.[97]

Auch in den 1990er Jahren existierte die Annahme, dass die Jastorfkultur als sozial und kulturell zusammengehörende Großgruppe bezeichnet werden kann aus der sich die Germanen herleiten lassen.[98] Allerdings seien neben der Jastorfkultur auch Kelten und südskandinavische Gruppen an der Ethnogenese „der" Germanen beteiligt gewesen bzw. der Kontakt zu den Kelten habe die germanische Ethnogenese erst ausgelöst.[99] Die Anwesenheit der Römer habe bei den Germanen zur Herausbildung eines Gemeinschaftsgefühls geführt.[100]

Die Problematik der ethnischen Deutung/Identifikation des Fundgutes mit ethnischen Gruppen ist so alt wie die Archäologie selbst. Um sich dem Thema zu nähern, soll zunächst geklärt werden, was eine Ethnie ist: Sie (die Ethnie) ist eine (Volks-) Gruppe mit einer einheitlichen materiellen und geistigen Kultur.[101] Zu einer einheitlichen Kultur zählt u. a. eine gemeinsame Sprache, der Glaube an eine gemeinsame Abstammung, gemeinsame Sitten und Traditionen.[102] Dieser Definition folgend, ist es also nach Ansicht einiger Forscher[103] möglich, anhand von materiellen Hinterlassenschaften festzustellen, ob deren einstige Besitzer eine gemeinsame

---

[93] PESCHEL, 1978, 22. Er sieht also die Germanen als Ethnie mit lokalen Besonderheiten.
[94] V. PETRIKOVITZ, 1986, 98.
[95] AMENT, 2003, 45.
[96] Vgl. PETRIKOVITZ, 1986.
[97] Nicht bei allen Autoren ist das eindeutig, aber aufgrund von Forschungstendenzen anzunehmen: NIERHAUS, 1966 u. a.
[98] M. SCHMIDT, Das Land der frühen Kelten und Germanen und der Mittelmeerraum (Frankfurt/ Main 1999), 333.
[99] SCHMIDT, 1999, 337 f.
[100] SCHMIDT, 1999, 338.
[101] www.duden.de. Als Archäologe kann man lediglich über die materielle Kultur urteilen. Alles weitere ist Spekulation.
[102] www.duden.de
[103] Vgl. SCHMIDT, 1999.

17

Sprache[104], den Glauben an eine gemeinsame Abstammung, ja ein Gemeinschaftsgefühl besessen hatten. Das übersteigt jedoch meines Erachtens die Aussagemöglichkeiten archäologischer Quellen bei Weitem. Archäologische Quellen zeigen einen Ausschnitt aus dem einstigen alltäglichen Leben.[105] Empfindungen, Zugehörigkeitsgefühle und Sprache sind mit archäologischen Methoden nicht zu rekonstruieren. Angenommen in einem bestimmten Gebiet kommen Schmuck- und Waffenfunde der gleichen Form und des gleichen Alters vor, spricht dennoch einiges gegen die Deutung, es handele sich deswegen um eine Ethnie. Ebenso ist es möglich, dass hier beispielsweise vier kulturell unterschiedliche Gruppen lebten, mit vier verschiedenen Sprachen und unterschiedlichen Traditionen. Durch die räumliche Nähe aber zu den anderen gleichen sich Schmuck- und Waffenformen. Dieser Umstand kann aber m. E. archäologische weder belegt noch widerlegt werden.

Es ist meiner Ansicht nach auch nicht möglich, Vermischungen von Sachgütern oder Anpassungen an bestehende kulturelle Gegebenheiten archäologisch zu fassen.

Eine unter Umständen existierende gewisse Einheitlichkeit der materiellen Kultur der Germanen ist m. E. nicht zurückzuführen auf einen gemeinsamen Ursprung, eine gemeinsame Identität, Sprache und Kultur, sondern, wie AMENT es treffend formuliert: Gemeinsamkeiten resultieren aus Ausgleichs- und Überschichtungsvorgängen. Einheitliche Lebensbedingungen, wie Klima und Vegetation, in Mitteleuropa führen zur Ausbildung übereinstimmender Wirtschaftsformen und Siedlungsweisen und ähnlichen sozialen Strukturen.[106]

---

[104] Dass eine einheitliche germanische Sprache existierte, gilt noch nicht einmal als gesichert!
[105] BRATHER, 2001, 33.
[106] AMENT, 2003, 46.

4. Völker zwischen Germanen und Kelten am Rhein - Theorien

Wie eingangs erwähnt, war das gemeinsame Werk von R. Hachmann, G. Kossack und H. Kuhn viele Jahrzehnte maßgebend in der Forschung und findet daher in dieser Arbeit besondere Beachtung. Die Methoden dieser Autoren sollen im Folgenden dargestellt und kritisch untersucht werden.

4. 1. ROLF HACHMANN – Der Rhein wird kulturelle Grenze

Archäologische Quellen

Das Arbeitsgebiet HACHMANNS liegt zwischen Lippe, Leine und mittleren Rhein. Zunächst stellt er in seiner Arbeit den archäologischen Sachverhalt dar und darauf folgend schriftliche Quellen. Er unternimmt einen neuen Lösungsversuch: Alle verschiedenen Quellen sollen erst einzeln und unabhängig voneinander analysiert und interpretiert werden. Die Interpretationsergebnisse stehen dann gleichwertig nebeneinander und werden anschließend kombiniert. Sinnvoll nach Auffassung HACHMANNS ist es, sich zuerst mit den archäologischen Quellen zu befassen. Wird mit den schriftlichen Quellen begonnen, könnte der Bearbeiter voreingenommen sein.[107] Seine Ergebnisse zu den archäologischen Quellen am Rhein sollen im folgenden Abschnitt vorgestellt werden:

Das Gebiet am Mittelrhein und im rheinischen Schiefergebirge[108], das eine weitgehend einheitliche Kultur (Abb. 2-4) zeigt, grenzt HACHMANN vorerst durch das Vorkommen von drei Erscheinungen der Latène-Kultur Süddeutschlands, des mittelfranzösischen Raumes und Böhmens ab.[109] Zum einen gibt es große Mengen von scheibengedrehter Ware östlich und westlich des Rheins. Allerdings dünnt ihr Vorkommen Richtung Norden aus (Abb. 5).[110] Auch handgefertigte Ware, die Ähnlichkeiten zu Typen aus dem nordfranzösischen Raum[111] aufweist, tritt gelegentlich auf.

---

[107] HACHMANN, 1962, 29.
[108] Wie bereits beschrieben, waren Lippe und Leine nördliche bzw. östliche Grenze. Wo Hachmann die südliche Grenze seines Arbeitsgebietes sieht, ist nicht bekannt.
[109] HACHMANN, 1962, 32.
[110] Ebd.
[111] Dieser ist allerdings kaum erforscht: HACHMANN, 1962, 32.

19

Zum anderen stellt HACHMANN unterschiedliche Kulturzonen anhand der Bestattungssitten heraus.[112] Sie sind zwar nicht einheitlich (sie zeigen lokale Sondererscheinungen), dennoch grenzt er aufgrund dieser Sondererscheinungen sein Gebiet von der Latène-Kultur ab.[113]

Auch die Siedlungsweise nutzt Hachmann zur Unterscheidung der verschiedenen Kulturzonen in seinem Arbeitsgebiet. Im Rheingebiet gibt es sowohl befestigte als auch unbefestigte Siedlungen. Einige Befestigungen boten der Bevölkerung wohl nur vorübergehend Schutz, wobei andere aufgrund ihrer Größe vermutlich für eine große Bevölkerungsgruppe längerfristigen Schutz bieten konnte.[114] Befestigte Großsiedlungen jedoch halten sich an die kulturellen Grenzen von Lippe und Leine.[115] Auch Münzfunde sind nördlich der Lippe und östlich der Leine nach HACHMANN nicht zu finden (Abb. 6).[116]

Er schlussfolgert daraus, dass generell durch Lippe und Leine zwei unterschiedliche Kulturgefüge getrennt werden. Sein Arbeitsgebiet zählt also im Wesentlichen zur Latène-Kultur. Aufgrund der Sondererscheinungen im keramischen Material, Bestattungssitten und Siedlungsformen, bezeichnet er es als „barbarisches Randgebiet" der Latène-Kultur.[117]

Gegen Mitte des ersten Jahrhunderts v. Chr. treten Fremderscheinungen auf, die auf die Wetterau beschränkt blieben. Anhand von Gräbern, Keramik- und Metallfunden soll das ersichtlich werden (Abb. 7). Diese Fremderscheinungen hatten keine unmittelbaren Vorläufer. Parallelen gibt es zur Przeworsk-Kultur (Abb. 8), die östlich von Oder und Neiße in Schlesien und Südpolen verbreitet war. Noch vor Ende des ersten Jahrhunderts v. Chr. verschwanden diese Fremderscheinungen wieder.[118]

Um Christi Geburt wird, Hachmann folgend, römischer Einfluss westlich des Rheins spürbar (Abb. 9). Östlich des Rheins stärkte die elbgermanische Kultur ihren Einfluss. Die einheimische Bevölkerung konnte ihnen nicht standhalten und übernahm deren Kultur. Da diese Einwanderer bäuerlich geprägt waren, wurden die

---

[112] HACHMANN, 1962, 32.
[113] Ebd.
[114] HACHMANN, 1962, 32. Zu solchen großen befestigten Siedlungen gibt Hachmann das Beispiel des so genannten Hunnenrings bei Otzenhausen im Saarland an. Es hat eine Fläche von 19 ha und gehört zur Gruppe der Oppida.
[115] HACHMANN, 1962, 33.
[116] Vgl. Anm. 78.
[117] HACHMANN, 1962, 35 f.
[118] HACHMANN, 1962, 36.

befestigten Siedlungen nicht genutzt, da sie diese nicht kannten.[119] Auch Gräberfelder wurden nicht weiter genutzt und eine lokale Münzprägung konnte ebenfalls nicht mehr nachgewiesen werden.[120] Der Rhein wurde zur scharfen Kulturgrenze.[121]

Mit anderen Worten: Im ersten Jahrhundert v. Chr. siedelten kulturell einheitliche/homogene Bevölkerungsgruppen westlich und östlich des Rheins, d. h. der Rhein ist als Grenze nicht wahrzunehmen.

Ab Christi Geburt trat eine Wandlung ein. Westlich des Rheins wirkte sich verstärkt römischer Einfluss aus, östlich des Flusses beeinflussten Elbgermanen die materielle Kultur.

Schriftquellen

Der erste, der Germanen als solche bezeichnete, war POSEIDONIUS VON APAMEIA um 90 v. Chr. Für ihn waren sie Teil der Kelten (Abb. 10). Bis dahin dachten Zeitgenossen, Kelten und Skythen teilen sich den nördlichen Erdkreis: den Nordosten bewohnten dabei die Skythen, den Nordwesten die Kelten (Dio. Cass. 53, 12). Ab wann Germanen als eine eigenständige Gruppe gesehen wurden ist nicht klar. Vermutlich erst mit den Berichten CAESARS.[122] Aus keltischer Sicht wurde CAESAR mitgeteilt, dass östlich des Rheins andersartige Menschen siedelten. Schon bei POSEIDONIUS galt der Rhein als (kulturelle) Grenze.[123] Auch CAESAR richtete sich nach der alten Gewohnheit, Flüsse als ethnische Grenzen anzusehen, denn noch bevor sich CAESAR über die ethnischen Verhältnisse klar war bezeichnete er den Rhein als Grenze.[124] Und obwohl er wusste, dass auch in Nordgallien Germanen ansässig waren, bezeichnete er den Rhein als Grenze.[125] Beispiel: Die Nervier haben Anspruch auf germanische Abstammung.[126]

Ansonsten ist nicht bekannt, dass die Bezeichnung *Germane* als Selbstbezeichnung benutzt wurde.[127] Er war wohl in Gebieten außerhalb des römischen Machtbereichs nicht üblich.[128]

---

[119] HACHMANN, 1962, 40 f.
[120] HACHMANN, 1962, 36.
[121] Ebd.
[122] HACHMANN, 1962, 44.
[123] Ebd.
[124] HACHMANN, 1962, 45.
[125] Ebd.
[126] Germ. Kap. 28.
[127] HACHMANN, 1962, 46.
[128] Ebd.

21

Aus Aufzeichnungen wohl von POSEIDONIUS, die bei STRABO erhalten geblieben sind, ist ebenfalls zu entnehmen, dass Germanen rechts des Rheins lebten (STRABO VII 290).[129]

Aus CAESARS Aufzeichnungen sind vor allem Aussagen für Gebiete am Niederrhein zu entnehmen (B. G. IV 1ff; VI 35; IV 16 ff.; V 35 ff.; VI 45; IV 3 ff.; VI 9 ff.).[130] Über Mittel- und Oberrhein trifft er kaum Aussagen. Tiefer im Landesinneren kannte CAESAR Sueben und Cherusker (B. G. IV 1 ff.; VI 9 ff.).[131]

Zusammenfassung

Welche Informationen können anhand der Auswertung der archäologischen Befunde und den Schriftquellen nach Hachmann gewonnen werden? Nach den Bodenfunden zu urteilen handelt es sich um Christi Geburt um „Grabsittenkreise", nach schriftlichen Quellen um „Kulturgenossenschaften".[132] Grabsittenkreise müssen mit den Kulturgenossenschaften nicht kongruent sein.[133] Aber für das erste Jahrhundert n. Chr. stimmen die Informationen aus archäologischen und schriftlichen Quellen überein.[134] Am Beispiel der suebischen „Kultgemeinschaft" wird dies deutlich: In den Gebieten an der Niederelbe zeigt sich eine archäologisch „einheitliche" Kultur, die durch die Schriftquellen bestätigt wird.[135] Die suebische Kultgemeinschaft entspricht also der elbgermanischen Kultur.[136] Auch die Zuwanderung suebischer Bevölkerungsteile ist archäologisch und historisch fassbar.[137] Dennoch sei zu beachten, dass nicht für jede Erwähnung von Sueben ein archäologischer Nachweis möglich ist und nicht jede archäologisch fassbare „Kultgemeinschaft" wurde in Schriftquellen erwähnt.[138]

Nach HACHMANN ist das Gesamtbild der ethnischen Verhältnisse am Rhein unklar, da der römische Germanenbegriff eine Anzahl von Gruppen umfasst, deren ethnischer Zusammenhang unklar ist.[139]

---

[129] Ebd. 48.
[130] Ebd. 10.
[131] Ebd.
[132] HACHMANN, 1962, 55 ff.
[133] HACHMANN, 1962, 56.
[134] Ebd. 60.
[135] Ebd. 77.
[136] Ebd. 55.
[137] Ebd. 56.
[138] Ebd.
[139] Ebd.

Kritik

HACHMANNS Methode, zuerst die archäologischen Quellen auszuwerten, ist meiner Meinung nach sinnvoll. Werden anfangs die Schriftquellen bearbeitet, besteht die Gefahr sich voreingenommen den archäologischen zu widmen. Doch die Auswertung des Quellenmaterials ist meiner Ansicht nach kritikwürdig. Sein Arbeitsgebiet ist im Westen durch den Mittelrhein, im Norden durch die Lippe und im Osten durch die Leine begrenzt.[140] Zwar zählt es nach HACHMANN zur Latène-Kultur, doch nimmt es aufgrund des archäologischen Materials eine Sonderstellung ein. Innerhalb dieses Gebietes vollzogen sich kulturelle Wandlungen: Im ersten Jahrhundert v. Chr. können, nach HACHMANN, weitgehend einheitliche kulturelle Erscheinungen festgestellt werden, sowohl westlich, als auch östlich des Rheins. HACHMANN will seine Theorie mit Hilfe der drei Fundgattungen Keramik, Bestattungen und Siedlungsform untermauern. Er stellt heraus, dass es in seinem Arbeitsgebiet massenhaft vorkommende scheibengedrehte Ware gäbe, was er als typisch für Latène-Gebiete (Abb. 5) bezeichnet.[141] Gelegentlich tritt handgefertigte Ware auf. Das Vorkommen beider Herstellungstechniken ist für HACHMANN ein Grund, sein Arbeitsgebiet abzugrenzen. Es stellt sich die Frage, ob in den anderen Latène-Gebieten handgefertigte Ware komplett fehlt, was meines Erachtens unwahrscheinlich ist. Vereinzelt konnten sicherlich Exemplare durch wandernde Gruppen bspw. auch in die Gebiete Süddeutschlands transportiert werden. Das ist zumindest nicht auszuschließen und allein deswegen ist dieser Punkt der HACHMANN'schen Argumentation zu verwerfen. Weiterhin ist das archäologische Material (Abb. 2-4) nicht geeignet, um seine Theorie zu bekräftigen. Die Abbildungen 2 und 3 zeigen das Fundinventar aus einer Kriegerbestattung von Wallertheim (Rheinhessen). Erstens gibt HACHMANN nicht an, worum es sich bei Abb. 2, 1-17 und Abb. 3, 1-10 handelt. Zweitens konnten keine Angaben ermittelt werden, warum die Funde spätlatènezeitlich datiert wurden. Auch Abbildung 4 gibt Rätsel auf, da wieder keine Angaben von HACHMANN existieren, worum es sich bei Abb. 4, 1-33 handelt. Ebenfalls führt er nicht aus, welche Keramik scheiben- oder handgefertigt ist, was aber wichtig ist, da er sein Argument mit diesen Abbildungen unterlegt. Und allein der technologische Aspekt (von Keramik) soll kulturelle

---

[140] Wo sich die südliche Grenze befindet, konnte nicht herausgefunden werden. Zu den Gebieten nördlich, nordwestlich und nordöstlich seines Arbeitsgebietes macht er zum kulturellen Habitus keine Angaben. Der Vergleich des Materials erfolgt nur zwischen seinem Arbeitsgebiet und den Gebieten der Latène-Kultur.
[141] HACHMANN, 1962, 32.

für dieses Jahrhundert die Hinweise aus den schriftlichen mit den aus den archäologischen Quellen übereinstimmen.

Abschließend ist festzuhalten, dass seine Methode und damit seine Hypothese nicht schlüssig und nicht nachvollziehbar sind und ein Überarbeiten seines Arbeitsgebietes zum Thema *Völker zwischen Germanen und Kelten am Rhein* erforderlich ist.

4. 2. GEORG KOSSACK – Die Verbreitung der Elbgermanen

KOSSACKS Arbeitsgebiet liegt zwischen Main und Nordsee. Im Wesentlichen stützt er sich auf die archäologischen Quellen. Die Untersuchungen der Schriftquellen fallen äußerst knapp aus.[150] Er bezieht sich auf CAESARS *De bello Gallico* und die *Germania* des TACITUS. Die einzigen Aussagen KOSSACKS zu *De bello Gallico* und *Germania* geben an, dass CAESAR tief greifende Unterschiede zwischen Kelten und Germanen hinsichtlich Religion, Kriegswesen, sozialer Ordnung etc. (B. G. VI 21 ff.) sieht und dass TACITUS sich den Ausführungen CAESARS anschließt. Generell liefern antike Schriften, so KOSSACK, kein sicheres Bild.[151]

Archäologische Quellen

Nach KOSSACKS Theorie herrschte in dem Gebiet zwischen Oberelbe und Main vor Christi Geburt eine keltische Kultur vor, die von germanischen Erscheinungen abgelöst wurde.[152] Erkennbar ist die Ablösung für KOSSACK im Wechsel des keramischen Fundguts um Christi Geburt. Germanische Keramik ist i. d. R. handgemacht, keltische Ware ist scheibengedreht (Abb. 12).[153] KOSSACK führt das auf einen Bevölkerungswechsel zurück. Auch wurden Oppida aufgegeben, heimisches Münzgeld verschwand. Die neue Bevölkerung ist Träger der archäologisch fassbaren elbgermanischen Kultur. Diese Kultur erkennt er anhand eines eimerartigen Gefäßes und einem bauchigen Topf mit Schrägrand (Abb. 12). Er bringt weiterhin das Frauengrab von Gladbach (Neuwied) als Beispiel an.[154]

Neben der elbgermanischen Kultur nimmt KOSSACK zwei weitere Gruppen an: eine Gruppe im Küstenbereich und eine Rhein-Weser-Gruppe (Abb. 13).[155] Diese drei

---

[150] KOSSACK, 1962, 85.
[151] Ebd. 76.
[152] Ebd. 75.
[153] Ebd. 83.
[154] Ebd. 85.
[155] Ebd. 77.

kulturellen Gruppen sind nach KOSSACK durch ähnliche Entwicklungen eine Einheit geworden; sie (die drei kulturellen Gruppen) sind nicht durch Spaltung einer Einheit entstanden. Im Laufe der Zeit haben sich bestimmte kulturelle Merkmale herausgebildet, die wir als germanisch betrachten.[156]

Kritik

KOSSACKS Argumentation ist nicht schlüssig und nicht ausreichend. Als erstes ist anzumerken, dass die strikte Einteilung von handgemachter und scheibengedrehter Keramik zu germanischer bzw. keltischer Kultur nicht sinnvoll ist. Es wird durchaus auch germanische Töpfer gegeben haben, die scheibengedrehte Ware nachgeahmt oder durch Handel erworben haben. Sicher ist auch nicht, dass nur keltische Töpfer das Handwerk mit der Töpferscheibe beherrschten. Außerdem ist die Herstellung der Keramik lediglich ein isoliertes typologisches Element, an dem allein keine Trennung verschiedener Kulturen konstatiert werden kann. KOSSACK stützt seine Argumentation auf lediglich zwei (!) Gefäße (Abb. 12). Da keine Vergleichsstücke präsentiert werden und keine Erklärung zu den Funden, zu Fundumständen und Datierungen abgegeben wurde, ist KOSSACKS Theorie nicht nachzuvollziehen.

Auch seiner Annahme zu den drei germanischen Gruppen, die sich zu einer Einheit entwickelt haben sollen, kann nicht zugestimmt werden. Zum einen bleibt unklar, wann sie existiert haben und zum anderen führt KOSSACK keine Argumente an, weder für ihre Existenz noch für die entstandene Einheit. Weiterhin werden überholte Erkenntnisse aus den 30er Jahren kritiklos übernommen.[157]

In seinem Fazit erklärt er, dass es Funde in seinem Arbeitsgebiet gibt, die weder germanisch noch keltisch sind. Er vermutet dort ein Gemisch aus Römern und Germanen.[158] Jedoch gibt es keinerlei Belege für seine Annahme oder weitere Erklärungen.

---

[156] Ebd. 77 f. Welche Merkmale damit gemeint sind, gibt KOSSACK nicht an.
[157] Zum Beispiel zitiert KOSSACK R. V. USLAR: KOSSACK, 1962, 75-85.
[158] KOSSACK, 1962, 85.

5. Fazit

Die Auswertung der schriftlichen Überlieferungen, *Commentarii de bello Gallico* und *De origine et situ Germanorum liber*, ergibt folgendes Bild: Wir erfahren von CAESAR, dass zu beiden Seiten des Rheins sowohl Gallier als auch Germanen gesiedelt haben. Es heißt, Germanen hätten zu Tausenden den Rhein überquert.[159] Dazu zählten Usipeter und Tencterer, die bei der Vertreibung durch die Menapier an das Westufer des Rheins gelangten.[160] Auch nennt CAESAR, und nur er, die Bezeichnung *Germani cisrhenani*, was soviel wie *linksrheinische Germanen* bedeutet.[161]

Ebenso hätten Gallier einst östlich des Rheins Kolonien besessen (B. G. VI, 24).

Problematisch an diesen Aussagen ist jedoch, dass nicht nachvollzogen werden kann, wann 15 000 Germanen den Rhein überschritten und wann Gallier östlich des Rheins gesiedelt haben sollen. So ist es nicht nachvollziehbar, ob diese Vorgänge in einem engeren Zeitraum geschehen sind, beispielsweise in einem Zeitraum von fünf Jahren oder ob diese gar nichts mehr miteinander zu tun haben.

Zwar gibt die Bezeichnung des Buches das Jahr an, jedoch ist anhand des Beispiels aus Buch VI unklar, wann Gallier östlich des Rheins Kolonien besaßen, auch wenn klar ist, dass das sechste Kriegsjahr, also 53 v. Chr. gemeint ist.

Letztendlich ist der Rhein nach den Aussagen CAESARS nicht als Grenze auszumachen. Aber die klare Einteilung der ansässigen Bevölkerung in Germanen und Kelten hat er vorgenommen. Andere Bezeichnungen für weitere Volksgruppen sind nicht überliefert.

Den Beschreibungen TACITUS' können wir entnehmen, dass er den Rhein als Westgrenze Germaniens (des freien Germaniens) wahrnahm.[162] Dennoch lebten wohl dort auch gallische Stämme östlich des Rheins[163], was m. E. bedeutet, dass er den Rhein als landschaftliche/ territoriale, nicht aber als kulturelle Grenze zwischen Germanen und Kelten betrachtete. So wird vielleicht auch die Bezeichnung *Germanien* als Bezeichnung eines Gebietes gemeint gewesen sein, nämlich des

---

[159] B. G. I, 31.
[160] B. G. IV, 1 und 4.
[161] NEUMANN, 1986, 107.
[162] Germ. Kap. 1.
[163] Germ. Kap. 28.

28

Gebietes zwischen Rhein, Donau, dem „Weltmeer" mit Dänemark und Skandinavien, sowie der Weichsel und Siebenbürgen.[164]

Auch TACITUS nimmt eine Zweiteilung in Germanen und Kelten vor ohne die Erwähnung andere Gruppen.

Beide Verfasser, Caesar und Tacitus, sahen die Gebiete des heutigen Frankreichs, der Beneluxstaaten und Deutschlands also besiedelt zum einen von Kelten, die wohl vorwiegend westlich des Rheins lebten und zum anderen von Germanen hauptsächlich östlich des Rheins. Aber als scharfe kulturelle Grenze kann der Fluss anhand der beiden schriftlichen Überlieferungen nicht angesehen werden.

Der archäologische Befund ist umstritten. Es gibt zahlreiche unterschiedliche Interpretationen der Funde am Rhein. Einmal wird angenommen, dass Träger der Jastorfkultur in die Gebiete östlich des Rheins vorgedrungen seien, wobei festgelegt wird, dass diese germanisch seien.[165] Ein Vordringen dieser Menschen über den Rhein kann aber archäologisch nicht belegt werden.[166]

Weiterhin gibt es Theorien, nach denen bereits um 700 v. Chr. Germanen östlich des Niederrheins siedelten, was mit dem Vorkommen von Urnengräbern und Bronzen(?) begründet wird.[167]

Ansonsten konnten kaum zuordenbare Funden gemacht werden. Nur Hachmann und Kossack stellen einige Funde vor, ansonsten findet man lediglich rein theoretische Ansätze zur Besiedlung des Rheins um Christi Geburt ohne Einbeziehung archäologischer Funde. Und anhand dieser sind keine Aussagen zu den Kernfragen möglich. Weder, ob der Rhein kulturelle Grenze war, noch ob es andere vermeintlich kulturell einheitliche Gruppen neben Germanen und Kelten gegeben hat.

Der Drang der Forschung, wie auch die Beispiele von HACHMANN und KOSSACK gezeigt haben, ist es die verschiedenen Quellengattungen zu synthetisieren. Auch wenn HACHMANN versucht hat, erst schriftliche und archäologische Quellen getrennt voneinander zu betrachten, so bleibt doch erkennbar, dass sie miteinander verknüpft wurden.[168] Aber genau das ist meiner Ansicht nach nicht abgebracht. Unterschiedliche Quellen beinhalten unterschiedliche Aussagen. Die germanischen

---

[164] Germ. Kap. 1. FUHRMANN, 2000, 71.
[165] V. PETRIKOVITZ, 1986, 98.
[166] Ebd.
[167] WAHLE, 1941a, 29.
[168] Siehe Kapitel 4. 1. *ROLF HACHMANN – Der Rhein wird kulturelle Grenze.*

Stämme, die in den Schriftquellen beschrieben werden, sind unter keinen Umständen mit archäologischen Funden in Verbindung zu bringen. Wenn CAESAR z. B. von den Ubiern berichtet, so ist doch anzunehmen, dass es sich um einen politischen Begriff handelt. Solch ein politischer Begriff sollte nicht schlichtweg mit einer kulturell einheitlichen Gruppe gleichgesetzt werden. Die Formulierung *kulturell einheitliche Gruppe* wurde deshalb gewählt, da sie das umfasst, was archäologische Funde im günstigsten Fall zeigen: eine Gruppe von Menschen mit unbekannter Anzahl an Personen, die gleiche Arten und Formen an materiellen Gütern, beispielsweise gleiche Keramikformen (Trichterbecher o. a.), aufweist. Und eben diese Gruppen können nicht mit politischen Bezeichnungen eines Caesars gleichgesetzt werden, da sich beide Bezeichnungen auf einen völlig unterschiedlichen Sachverhalt beziehen und in einem anderen Kontext stehen, wie Brather es treffend formuliert hat: Schriftliche Quellen berichten v. a. über politische Ereignisse und Prozesse, handeln von Personen, Vorstellungen und Wahrnehmungen der Zeitgenossen. Archäologische Quellen zeigen einen Ausschnitt aus dem alltäglichen Leben.[169]

Meiner Ansicht nach, sollte auch in Zukunft davon Abstand genommen werden, unterschiedliche Quellengattungen miteinander verknüpfen zu wollen. Eine Zusammenarbeit von Historikern, Archäologen u. a. ist zwar sinnvoll, aber in der Hinsicht, Wissen und Erfahrungen auszutauschen und nicht Erkenntnisse zwanghaft verknüpfen, um unter allen Umständen ein eindeutige Ergebnisse erhalten zu wollen.

---

[169] BRATHER, 2001, 33.

6. Verzeichnisse

6. 1. Quellen- und Literaturverzeichnis

QUELLENVERZEICHNIS:

G. I. CAESAR	M. DEISSMANN, De bello Gallico. Lateinisch-Deutsch (Stuttgart 1995).
P. C. TACITUS	M. FUHRMANN, P. Cornelius Tacitus – Germania (Stuttgart 2000).

LITERATURVERZEICHNIS:

AMENT 2003	H. AMENT, Unterwegs zu höherer Zivilisation – Die Germanen. In: W. SCHULLER, Frühe Völker Europas (Stuttgart 2003).
BRATHER 2001	S. BRATHER, Archäologie der westlichen Slawen (Berlin/ New York 2001).
HACHMANN 1962	R. HACHMANN, Germanen und Kelten am Rhein in der Zeit um Christi Geburt. In: R. HACHMANN, G. KOSSACK, H. KUHN, Völker zwischen Germanen und Kelten (Neumünster 1962).
JANKUHN 1977	H. JANKUHN, Einführung in die Siedlungsarchäologie (Berlin/ New York 1977).
JANKUHN 1986	H. JANKUHN, Das Germanenproblem in der älteren archäologischen Forschung. In: H. BECK (Hrsg.), Germanenprobleme in heutiger Sicht (Berlin/ New York 1986).
KOSSACK 1962	G. KOSSACK, Archäologisches zur frühgermanischen Besiedlung zwischen Main und Nordsee. In: R. HACHMANN, G. KOSSACK, H. KUHN, Völker zwischen Germanen und Kelten (Neumünster 1962).
KOSSINNA 1881	G. KOSSINNA, Über die ältesten hochfränkischen Sprachdenkmäler – Ein Beitrag zur Grammatik des

Althochdeutschen (veröffentlichte Dissertation),
(Straßburg 1881).

Kossinna 1920   G. Kossinna, Die Herkunft der Germanen. Zur
Methode der Siedlungsarchäologie (Leipzig 1920).

Lund 1986   A. A. Lund, Zum Germanenbegriff bei Tacitus. In: H.
Beck (Hrsg.), Germanenprobleme in heutiger Sicht
(Berlin/ New York 1986).

Mildenberger 1986   G. Mildenberger, Die Germanen in der
archäologischen Forschung nach Kossinna. In: H. Beck
(Hrsg.), Germanenprobleme in heutiger Sicht (Berlin/
New York 1986).

Nierhaus 1966   R. Nierhaus, Das suebische Gräberfeld von
Diersheim. In: Römische – Germanische Forschungen,
28 (Berlin 1966), 182-234.

Neumann 1986   G. Neumann, Germani cisrhenani – die Aussage der
Namen. In: H. Beck (Hrsg.), Germanenprobleme in
heutiger Sicht (Berlin/ New York 1986).

Peschel 1978   K. Peschel, Anfänge germanischer Besiedlung im
Mittelgebirgsraum. In: Arbeits- und Forschungsberichte
zur sächsischen Bodendenkmalpflege, 12 (Berlin
1978), 5-153.

Peschel 1988   K. Peschel, Kelten und Germanen während der
jüngeren vorrömischen Eisenzeit (2.-1. Jahrhundert v.
Chr.). In: F. Horst/ F. Schlette (Hrsg.), Frühe Völker
in Mitteleuropa (Berlin 1988), 167-200.

Schmidt 1999   M. Schmidt, Das Land der frühen Kelten und
Germanen und der Mittelmeerraum (Frankfurt/ Main
1999).

Schumacher 1921   K. Schumacher, Siedlungs- und Kulturgeschichte der
Rheinlande von der Urzeit bis in das Mittelalter (Mainz
1921).

Von Petrikovitz 1986   H. v. Petrikovitz, Germani cisrhenani. In: H. Beck
(Hrsg.), Germanenprobleme in heutiger Sicht (Berlin/
New York 1986).

VON USLAR 1938   R. VON USLAR, Westgermanische Bodenfunde. In:
                       Römisch-Germanische Kommission (Hrsg.),
                       Germanische Denkmäler der Frühzeit (Berlin 1938),
                       173-183.

WAHLE 1941 a   E. WAHLE, Zur ethnischen Deutung frühgeschichtlicher
                       Kulturprovinzen (Heidelberg 1941).

WAHLE 1941 b   E. WAHLE, Grenzen der frühgeschichtlichen Erkenntnis
                       (Heidelberg 1941).

WAHLE 1952   E. WAHLE, Deutsche Vorzeit (Basel 1952).

ZEITLER 1986   W. M. ZEITLER, Zum Germanenbegriff Caesars. In: H.
                       BECK (Hrsg.), Germanenprobleme in heutiger Sicht
                       (Berlin/ New York 1986).

6. 2. Abbildungsverzeichnis

7. Abbildungen

Abbildung 1: Die Stammesverteilung im nordwestlichen Germanien im 1. Jh. n. Chr.

Abbildung 2: Kriegerbestattung der Spätlatènezeit von   Nauheim. Wallertheim (Rheinhessen), Grab 3.

34

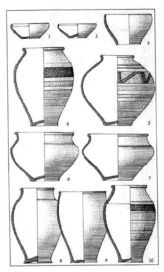

Abbildung 3: Keramik aus der Kriegerbestattung von Wallertheim (Rheinhessen)

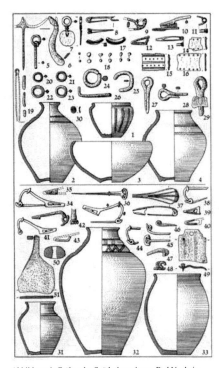

Abbildung 4: Gräber der Spätlatènezeit von Bad Nauheim

35

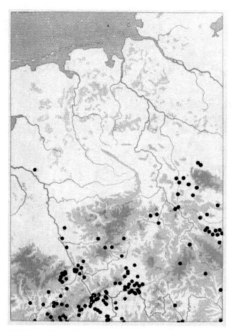

Abbildung 5: Verteilung der Drehscheibenkeramik.

Abbildung 6: Verteilung spätkeltischer Münzen zwischen Rhein und Weser.

36

Abbildung 7: Gräber der Spätlatènezeit mit „ostgermanischem" Inventar aus der Wetterau.

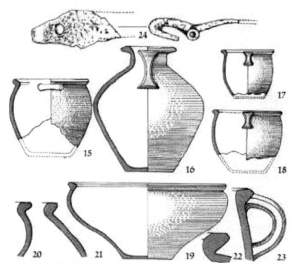

Abbildung 8: Gräber der Spätlatènezeit mit „ostgermanischem" Inventar aus Posen.

37

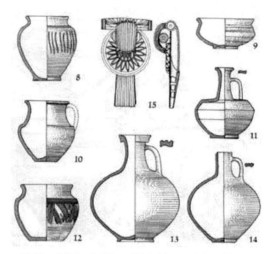

Abbildung 9: Gräber der Zeit um Christi Geburt an Rhein und Saar.

Abbildung 10: Besiedlung Mitteleuropas in der 1. Hälfte des 1. Jh. v. Chr.

38

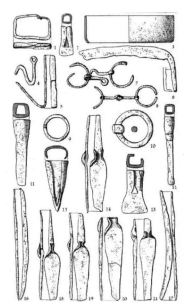

Abbildung 11: Hortfund der Spätlatènezeit von Kalteiche (Dillkreis).

Abbildung 12: Gräber aus der Zeit um Christi Geburt aus Holstein, Niedersachsen, Brandenburg und Böhmen

39

Abbildung 13: Germanische Fundgruppen der römischen Kaiserzeit zwischen Elbe und Rhein.
○Elbgermanen ⊠Nordseegermanen ●Rhein-Weser-Germanen ‖ Provinzialrömisches Gebiet